MW00582312

THE MIDAS OF MANUMISSION

THE ORPHAN SAMUEL GIST AND HIS VIRGINIAN SLAVES

Barb Drummond

barbdrummond.com

ISBN: 978-1-912829-03-3 ebook

978-1-912829-04-0 paperback

978-1-912829-05-7 hardback

By the same author:

Mr Bridges' Enlightenment Machine - Forty Years on Tour in Georgian England

Frolicksome Women & Troublesome Wives - wife Selling in England

This book is dedicated to Paul Turner who has worked so hard to preserve the legacy that Gist left his former slaves. It is also dedicated to all the other descendants of the Gist freedmen and freedwomen.

I also wish to thank Paula 'Kitty' Wright for her book 'Gist's Promised Land' and her encouragement to me in writing this book to expand the story to encompass events on both sides of the Atlantic.

Virginia was to be planted primarily for the enrichment of English investors, not for the development of America. Most of those emigrating were in effect slaves, though in name servants.

England, from her geographical position and the paucity of shipping, had been aloof from European influences to a surprising degree. But she had worked out during the Middle Ages an extension of liberty to her people... Thomas Smith's fellow-countrymen [were] almost fanatical in their attitude toward unfettered right to live as they pleased.
    E. Keble Chatterton

CONTENTS

INTRODUCTION

The story of Samuel Gist appeared amidst this author's research into Britain's Abolition of the African slave trade, to celebrate and commemorate its bicentenary in 2007. It began with the discovery of a small item in the Bristol press announcing the death of Samuel Gist in London. He had left a large legacy to his former school, Queen Elizabeth's Hospital, and also freed a large number of his slaves in Virginia.

Bristol was a major port for the slave trade in the early decades of the eighteenth century. But Gist's story widened the tale to involve natives of the city actually owning slaves in North America. It also hinted that Gist might represent the much sought after historians' equivalent of the philosopher's stone: a man involved in slavery who had had a change of heart, an epiphany, and who had used his money from the trade to help its victims.

A further strand was added to this already complex tapestry with the discovery that descendants of his freed slaves exist, a living legacy of this forgotten Englishman. But the freeing of their ancestors failed to provide a happy ending, as there were so many legal and financial obstacles to overcome at the time, and the after effects continue to reverberate.

Samuel Gist is claimed to have been an orphan, which adds yet another element to this story. Orphans are common in our history and literature, from Moses to Mowgli, Cinderella to Harry Potter, Nelson Mandela, Mata Hari, Romulus and Remus, St Nicholas, Alexander Hamilton and Malcolm X, Marie Curie, Charles Darwin, Ada Lovelace, Newton, Dampier, Nelson, Bligh and no less than five prime ministers of Australia. Orphans are often included in fiction to demonstrate a character's early suffering and their society's support — or lack of it — for the young and vulnerable. They can also be used to celebrate victory over adversity. This huge list also highlights a much overlooked element of human history: that of children and childcare. Without children, society cannot continue, so a world in which they are neglected must be considered seriously dysfunctional and possibly doomed.

Details of Samuel's early life are unclear, but with high infant mortality of up to 60%, his survival into his ninety-second year alone is striking. Though he did not spend his childhood begging on the streets of Bristol as some people in North America claim, his early life must have been a struggle. His rise to great wealth on two continents was spectacular, but it coincided with the expansion of trade and commerce on both sides of the Atlantic, so his story reflects many aspects of the age. But his decision to free so many slaves in Virginia was unprecedented, and his motives have been the source of debate in the ensuring centuries.

Another problem in this story is the huge amount of contradictory and often inaccurate information which had been given wider distribution through modern media. His story is also littered with inaccurate records. A book published in Chicago in 1883 wrongly described Gist as a banker, and the account was unclear on whether he ever visited North America or saw a single slave. It also claimed he had only one daughter, that he owned one thousand slaves and that nine hundred settled in Brown County,[1] all of which are wrong.

Another imaginative version of his life is from Elsie Johnson Ayres.[2] She claims he owned thousands of acres of English countryside, his house at Wormington Grange was built by him and its entrance hall was "lined with portraits of ancestors done by some of the leading artists",[3] so she missed the part of his story that he was an orphan. She describes barns to house the fine racehorses which were Gist's main hobby. This is pure fiction and seems to be based on various claims that he imported the first Arabian racehorses to North America, which would be impressive, but he was still a schoolboy in England at the time this happened, a detail overlooked by many other writers. She also claims he was a "sea faring man", which is also nonsense. Then she claims "After going through countless English histories and old records in Richmond Virginia it has definitely been found to be a historical fact that Samuel Gist made his great fortune trafficking in slaves".[4] From this invention, she concludes his slaves believed the manumission, or freeing of his slaves, was due to his troubled conscience, "because of his nefarious activities as a slave trader".[5] She also claims Samuel never visited the United States.

Gist had a tough start in life as an orphan in a city infamous at the time for political corruption and its heavy involvement in the African slave trade. His education was paid for out of charity before he was sent as an apprentice to a strange land. Yet he became a business partner of George Washington, and a significant merchant, insurance broker and landowner in both Virginia and England, from which he made several fortunes. After the War of Independence, he pursued his North American debtors with ferocity, and apparently exploited relatives. His hard-nosed business practices earned him many enemies. Yet he was a generous patron of many charities, and his former slaves spoke fondly of him.

So it seems the man and what drove him were complicated. This book aims to shed some light on the life of this enigmatic man, and on the world he lived in, on both sides of the Atlantic in the eighteenth century

1

BRISTOL

Samuel Gist was born in Bristol in the early eighteenth century, but for unknown reasons his name was spelled differently from theirs. The name Guest can be found in the city and its hinterland, but his date of birth cannot be established. Some sources claim he came from the parish of Temple, but the church registers have been lost and the copy — preserved as the Bishop's Transcript — is largely illegible for this period. Records of men becoming burgesses, i.e. freemen permitted to run businesses and to vote in the city, include a John Guest who was granted his freedom of the city in 1713 after completing his apprenticeship with Richard Long, a weaver in Temple parish. This means John Guest was at least twenty-one years old, so was born in or before 1692. A Thomas Guest became a burgess as a weaver in 1723, so he may have been John's younger brother or a cousin. The accounts for Queen Elizabeth's Hospital school record that Samuel Guest was admitted in 1733 as the son of John Guest of St Phillips. Boys were admitted at the age of ten, which dates Samuel's birth to 1723 or earlier.

St Phillip's parish was separated from Temple by the River Avon. It was on the edge of the city so boasted shops and businesses and a wide road, Old Market, where trade was carried out beyond the control of the city. It had allegedly included a market centuries earlier where English slaves were sold and shipped to Ireland. By the time Samuel was born, the area had become infamous for drunkenness and disorderly behaviour at its annual fair on West Street. The parish was huge: extending about halfway to Bath, so it took in a vast area of countryside, including the coal mining region of Kingswood.

But there were few gentry in residence to help care for the poor, so when famines struck the region in the eighteenth century, hungry locals often rioted in Bristol. The best known resident was Norborne Berkeley of Stoke Park; he was part of a West Country family heavily involved in early North American settlement. After running into financial problems in 1768, he was appointed Governor of Virginia; like many before him, he fled to the colonies in search of a fresh start.

The River Avon runs through the city; in mediaeval times, wealthy merchants' houses lined its banks, allowing them to load their ships directly from the warehouses which were part of their homes. By the early eighteenth century, wealth was mostly concentrated on the northern bank and in the old city centre. The southern region was comprised of the parishes of St Thomas and Temple, which had long associations with the wool trade, and early maps show large open spaces where woollen cloth was stretched on tenter hooks to dry them after dyeing. Temple church dated from the fourteenth century; it was famous for its tower which leaned due to it being built on waterlogged ground. It had an ornate chapel dedicated to St Katherine, patron saint of weavers, which dated from 1299.[1]

The importance of the weaving trade to the city is shown by a city ordinance from the time of Edward IV, quoted without alteration:

"on Seynt Kateryne's even [November 4th] the maire and sherif and their brethren [are] to walk to Seynt Katheryn's chapell within Temple church, there to heare theire evensong, and ... to walke unto the Kateryn hall, [the weaver's guildhall] there to be worshipfully received of the wardeyns and brethern of the same; and in the halle there to have theire fires, and their drynkyngs, with spysid cake-brede and sondry wynes; the cuppes merelly filled about the house, and then do depart every man home; the mayre, sherif, and the worshipfull men redy to receyve at their dores Seynt Kateryn's players, making them to drynk at their dores, and rewardyng theym for theire playes. And on the morrowe, Seynt Kateryn's day, the maire, sherif, and their brethern to be at the Temple churche, there to hire masse and offre. And then every man retray home."[2]

Weaving's importance is also shown by the number of words and metaphors in English that still refer to it, second only to agriculture. They include 'spin a yarn', which also suggests story telling accompanied groups of women spinning together. 'Unravel a mystery', 'web of life', 'fine-drawn' which meant a cloth was so fine it could be drawn through a ring. Home spun is self explanatory, and tease refers to the teasels, a form of thistle that was used to raise the knap on the woven cloth. And of course, the professional spinner: 'a spinster'.

But there is an even more modern inclusion in our language, from Scotland.

"On moonlight nights [people of Lowland Scotland] had their gatherings in the evening, when, with music, singing and dancing, they also enacted the story of some old song, little dramas, not too refined in which they showed what rustic skill and rude humour they could. On moonlight nights they held their favourite meetings in barn or cottage, called 'Rockings', when young women brought their rocks and reels, or distaffs and spindles — where young men assembled, and to the accompaniment of the spinning of the wool and flax the song and merriment went round, till the company dispersed, and girls went home escorted by their swains, who carried gallantly their rocks over corn-rigs and moor. When 'rocks' were no more used, and spinning-wheels had taken their place, still by the familiar name of 'rockings' were these merry social meetings called."[3]

It seems the cloth trade gave us the name for modern popular music.

The Weavers' Guild declined to the extent it could no longer maintain the hall by 1786, so it became a synagogue,[4] before being demolished a few decades later.

Spinning was practised by women; for single women this was often their only source of labour, hence they were called spinsters. It helped pass the long winter months; men did the weaving, and the home industry was organised by employers or middlemen. Woollen cloth made up 40% of English exports, and great efforts were invested in promoting woollen cloth at home and abroad. Following the Restoration, when Charles II re-introduced European style luxury, woollen clothing became unfashionable amongst the elite, so to shore up the industry, a series of Burial in Wool Acts were passed in 1666–80. All shrouds were to be made of wool, except for the bodies of plague victims or the poor whose burials were paid for by their local parishes. Certificates to this effect were signed by parish officers; breaking the law incurred a fine of five pounds.

Cloth manufacture was as important to Britain as corn growing, and Parliament protected both. "It forbade the import of foreign cloth and the export of raw wool, killed the Irish cloth trade for the benefit of the English clothiers."[5] Gibraltar was taken in 1704 to ensure wool could still be traded in the Mediterranean in return for olive oil which was essential for its manufacture. Major export markets included Spain, the American colonies and Russia. Only the Far East was not interested.[6]

Wool had been traded with the great seafaring Venetians, but this ended in the mid- sixteenth century when the Italian city states were ruined by the increasing dangers of overland routes to the east which had inspired the establishment of sea routes via South Africa. But:

"In 1587 the last of the argosies sent by Venice to Southampton

was wrecked off the Needles: with her sank the mediaeval system
of trade and all that it meant to Italy and to England."[7]

The cloth trade in the Middle Ages was based on the guild
system, in which training was controlled and rules enforced by each
city. But this system was inflexible when ships abandoned Europe for
the more higher risk long distance routes to Asia and the Americas,
so trading became more open, and involved merchant capitalists.[8]
One of the most successful of these groups was Bristol's *Society of
Merchant Venturers* who travelled abroad to trade, and owned and
shared the risk of each other's vessels and goods. When trade with
the Americas expanded, they were in the best position both
geographically and economically to profit from it. In the past, mediaeval England had been "traded with" by Italians, French and
Germans. Elizabethan England was excluded from trade with
Catholic Europeans, so sought markets further afield. "Commer-
cially we had ceased to be the anvil; we had become the hammer."[9]

The Spanish Armada's failed invasion established England's
naval superiority after her navy prevented the Spanish invading
these islands. But Sir Francis Drake had no interest in claiming
Spain or her colonies. In mainland Europe, armies were the main
source of defence for the nation, and could be turned on common-
ers, to maintain authority, but in Britain, the main national defence
was the navy. The English army could be raised and disbanded
when required, but ships required huge investment, beyond the
reach of monarchs, so they relied on merchants to provide ships and
skilled manpower.

"The Navy does not enable a monarch to hold down its subjects,
as a royal army may do. In England there was no Royal Army and
in the Civil War of Charles I, the navy took the side of
Parliament."[10]

At its height, the slave trade was defended on the grounds that it
was the nursery of the navy; it kept sailors employed and ships
afloat so they could be converted in time of war.

Before the Reformation, sailors fought for their god and their nation, but the Tudors put themselves at the head of the Church and sold off many of its properties. Mammon replaced faith, as Sir Walter Raleigh wrote:

"All discourse of magnanimity, or national virtue, of religion or liberty and whatsoever else hath been wont to move and encourage virtuous men, hath no force at all with the common soldier in comparison of spoil and riches; the rich ships are boarded upon all disadvantages, the rich towns are furiously assaulted, and the plentiful countries willingly invaded. Our English nations have attempted many places in the Indies, and run upon the Spanish headlong in hopes of their reals, of plate and pistolets, which, had they been put to it on the like disadvantages in Ireland or in any poor country, they would have turned their pieces and pikes against their commanders."[11]

But by the early eighteenth century, the southern region of Bristol, i.e. the former cloth-making suburb, was in long-term decline. Fine merchants' houses were decaying and converted into small factories and tenements for immigrants fleeing rural poverty — mostly in Somerset — in search of work. It was an unhealthy area, prone to flooding and many residents were in need of charity. The Elizabethan Poor Laws made parishes responsible for their own poor. This meant that each parish acted as a guild; membership was by birth, or it could be purchased. In 1727 a Mr Newby applied to live in the riverside parish of St Mary le Port in Bristol. But he had to provide guarantees that his family would not become a burden on the parish, so he and his friends had to provide a bond of forty pounds.[12] But by the late seventeenth century, the system was failing as the rich and poor no longer lived together as neighbours. Attempts were made to encourage the richer parishes to support the densely populated poor regions such as St James, Castle Precincts, Temple and St Thomas. John Carey proposed the city build a central poorhouse in St Peter's parish to house the needy more efficiently.

By the time Samuel was born, the weaving and dyeing industries were vanishing, and there was little work to replace them. In 1709 the government asked Bristol Corporation to accept some Protestant Refugees from German states, but the request was refused. The corporation claimed the city had almost no manufacturers and that both locals and French refugees (Huguenots) were all out of work.[13] A collection of fifteen thousand pounds was benevolently raised in London to send them to Ireland and North America. This lack of sympathy for foreigners was again shown when Bristol MP's voted against the Naturalisation of Foreign Protestants Bill in 1750, and in 1753, they opposed the naturalisation of Jews.[14]

Speculating in essential foodstuffs began to undermine the tradition of fair trading, and ensuring food was affordable for the poor. In 1708 the Kingswood colliers came to Bristol to object to the rising price of wheat. The unrest was quelled when magistrates forced sellers to reduce their prices. The colliers rioted again in 1752, and in 1765, vessels loaded with grain were banned from leaving the port.[15] The harvests of 1728 and '29 were poor, which led to rising crime, especially late night robberies on the city streets. Nearly two hundred shiploads of grain had to be imported, some from New York and Philadelphia for the first time. Wages for weavers were reduced by masters, which triggered widespread rioting, burning of looms and the destruction of several masters' houses. A number of rioters were sentenced to death. The press gang was also active, seizing men off the streets to serve in the navy.[16]

The Restoration of the monarchy in 1660 led to the Stuart kings selling trade monopolies to London guilds, which in turn increased London's dominance over the provinces. Even the postal system was London-based, with all post having to be sent via the capital, a hopelessly time-wasting system. By 1700 over a tenth of the nation's five and a half million inhabitants lived in the city. Bristol and her long-time rival Norwich were second with thirty thousand each. But the introduction of a series of Navigation Acts, which forced colonies to use only British ships, caused a decline in the eastern ports trading with Europe, in favour of the Western ports, especially those of the south-west such as Plymouth and Bristol.[17] Bristol also had an extensive hinterland, linked by land and via the River Severn, so was uniquely independent of London.

For centuries Bristol had been a flourishing port, far enough inland to protect it from raiders. The River Avon has the second highest tidal range in the world, which drove ships to the safety of the city's quays. Daniel Defoe praised the crowded quays and flourishing trade, but complained that the city could have been much bigger if buildings had been allowed beyond the city walls. But these same walls ensured taxes were collected from traders attending markets and fairs, so they were a reliable source of income for the city.

When the American and Caribbean colonies were established, Bristol flourished by providing them with a wide range of goods from salted beef to house bricks, furniture and clothing. It was also a major port of departure for people heading to the colonies, either as immigrants or as soldiers to fight the many wars with Britain's European neighbours, especially France and Spain. Bristol's huge fairs attracted traders from Ireland and Wales, and towns to the north along the River Severn, from London and even Europe, so was a major site for the exchange of local and international goods. In the eighteenth century the annual St James' fair was shifted to coincide with the return of the West Indies fleet, reflecting how important this event had become both for the city's trade and to celebrate the safe return of local sailors.

Following the closure of the monasteries by Henry VIII, no arrangements had been made to replace their role in the care of the poor, aged and infirm. Religious houses had provided a pool of celibate people which had acted as a brake on population, so the Tudor age saw an explosion in the birth rate, especially among the poor. Queen Elizabeth was forced to take steps such as encouraging the better-off to take in poor children, to aid young couples to set up house, and to fund their businesses. Guardians of the Poor advertised children — often described as plump and healthy — as apprentices, effectively selling them to remove them from being a liability on the parish. Parishes were made responsible for the poor in their area, and before the Reformation, this role had been paid for out of tithes, but these were now diverted to support the newly married clergy and their families. Poor rates were introduced, but were widely resented and difficult to collect as an additional form of taxation. Draconian laws were introduced to control idlers, beggars and thieves.

Merchants were encouraged to establish and fund charities, and some bequeathed money in their wills, echoing the pre-Reformation practice of establishing chantries which paid for priests and the grateful poor to pray for their souls to reduce their time in purgatory. These same priests often had time to run schools for the poor, so when Henry VIII abolished these charities, he also put an end to most educational funding. In many towns and cities, new schools had to be established to educate and care for the poor, and almshouses for the elderly and infirm. In Bristol, two city schools were established. Bristol Grammar was founded by Royal Charter in 1532 and funded by Nicholas and Robert Thorne. Its aim was to educate the sons of Bristol merchants and tradesmen prior to them becoming apprentices. Most went to the sea, but a few high-flyers also went to Oxford.

John Carr died in 1586 and in his will left funds from the rents of his Congresbury estate to establish a school for "men children whose parents are deceased or dead or fallen into decay and not able to relieve them"[18] who came from the city of Bristol and his manor. In 1587 Bristol Corporation obtained a private Act of Parliament to carry out his wishes.

Despite local loyalties and familial networks, wealthy merchants were a small group, and frequently married and traded over great distances, often via London. John Carr's father William was from Ipswich, but served as Bristol's mayor and MP. John lived in Bristol and Stratford by Bow, now part of London. He invented a process for making white soap – a huge improvement on the coarse impure form in use at the time, so this was probably the basis of his great fortune.[19] It was called Queen Elizabeth's Hospital in honour of the monarch, but it was not a hospital in the modern sense. The term originally referred to a place of rest and accommodation for pilgrims, many of whom travelled in search of cures, so they sometimes required healthcare and occasionally died. When pilgrimages were abolished by Henry VIII the charities evolved in response to local needs. The new Anglican clerics were allowed to marry, so some of their widows and orphans became destitute, and some hospitals cared for them. The children were educated there, and as other charities were founded to care for the poor and invalids, some hospitals become schools.

Queen Elizabeth's Hospital was modelled on London's Christchurch Hospital, and its governors were members of the Bristol Corporation (council). It opened in 1590 after the Governors obtained the former Hospital of the Gaunts', a crumbling cloister and church opposite the Cathedral on College Green. It was just outside the city walls, near the docks but on high ground, so it survived the tsunami which devastated Wales and the West Country in 1703. In this church is a memorial to a young orphan who died in 1627; he is dressed in fine clothes with a lace ruff, kneeling piously.

Children are almost unknown on monuments except when lined up in prayer beneath their late parents, so this boy was special. He was John Cooke, son and heir of Vincent Cooke of Hifield Esq. Though not named as such, he was probably a pupil at Queen Elizabeth's Hospital, as this was their chapel. If so, this suggests that the school was far from providing shelter for starving waifs, the school more often educated the children of well-to-do locals who lacked relatives able or willing to take them in after the death of one or both of the child's parents died. Thus Samuel Gist was probably not the ragged waif of popular literature. Nor did he, as some American sources claim, spend his time begging in the streets. Though the regime, with boys rising at five every morning, even in winter, seems harsh, such hours were normal at the time to maximise the limited hours of daylight.

Nothing is known of Samuel's mother, but in his will, he mentioned several cousins with the surname of Rogers, some of whom were listed in southern parish registers, including Temple. It was also the name of an important local and national family. From the late seventeenth century Britain was often at war with her neighbours, especially the French and Spanish in disputes over the Caribbean and North American colonies. The Spaniards brought galleons laden with spice from the east, and silver from South America, which were tempting prizes for British sailors.

In 1708 several Bristol merchants and ship owners — mostly members of the Quakers but also a Francis Rogers — invested in two ships, one of which was captained by Woodes Rogers. The other was captained by the former buccaneer and diarist William Dampier who was navigator for both. Though little known today, he was involved in an astounding number of major historical events. He was the first man to circumnavigate the globe three times, and his resulting maps were used by Captain Cook on his explorations of the South Seas. Rogers and Dampier led raids on several ships including one of the Spanish treasure ships, before stopping for water at Juan Fernandez Island where the castaway Alexander Selkirk was rescued and who went on to publish a popular account of his life there. Rogers later vanquished a group of pirates in the Bahamas and established a colony where he became the governor and lived until his death.[20] He is commemorated with a plaque on one of his former houses on Queen Square in central Bristol.

The peculiarly English practice of sending children to be raised by strangers — either at boarding schools or via apprenticeships — was a continuation of the custom from the unstable mediaeval times and earlier, when the sons of wealthy families would be sent to live with allies or trading partners. They learned new skills, but the practice was also a way to build trust between the families; if they fell out the boys could be used as hostages to avert war. In the eighteenth century, many sons of merchants were sent abroad to learn local languages and practices, which widened the young man's outlook and helped build allegiances and trust. A letter in the Bristol press from the 1750s complained of the decline in this practice, which meant that many merchants trading abroad were less well informed of local conditions, and so less able to cope with problems. Gist's relocation to Virginia may have been part of this tradition of long distance training in skills and diplomacy.

Most boys whose families were in businesses or trades in towns acquired a basic education starting at the age of seven, from their family, or a tutor if they could afford it. They were apprenticed at about fourteen and were fully qualified as tradesmen or journeymen when they came of age, at twenty-one, when they could marry and set up in business. This paved the way for the establishment of boarding schools in the nineteenth century which were largely to train boys for service in the far-flung lands of the empire.

Girls often went into domestic service at an early age, which allowed them to save up to provide themselves with a dowry, as families — especially if they had several children — often lacked the funds to do so. The average age of marriage was the mid- to late-twenties, suggesting it took several years for young people to save up enough to marry But low wages in the countryside became such a problem that by the mid-eighteenth century, many areas had too few hands to bring in the harvest, which raised the risks of famines. An article in the press of 1766 suggested that instead of rural charities paying for boys to be apprenticed, the money should be spent on providing dowries for poor girls to marry, to keep young people in the countryside, and to produce future generations.[21] The alternative of providing a living wage — then, as now — seems not to have been an option.

At the dawn of the eighteenth century, the city of Bristol — though damaged badly in the Civil War — was still largely enclosed by its walls, and many buildings were little changed since the Middle Ages. The annalist John Latimer mocked its people for being "as illiterate as the back of a tombstone".[22] Few people owned books beyond a family Bible and perhaps *The Book of Common Prayer*. The first parish school was founded in Temple in 1709 and largely funded by wealthy philanthropist Edward Colston who founded Colston's Hospital in 1700 to educate one hundred poor boys. There were also several private writing schools. Sons of the wealthy were educated by private tutors, often to prepare them to attend one of England's two universities.

If young Samuel was born in Temple parish, it seems logical that he would have attended the parish school, but it was only for the poor of the parish, suggesting he was not one of them. Latimer claimed the boys of Queen Elizabeth's Hospital received the minimum of schooling. The school claimed the boys were to be "educated according to the limits of their abilities",[23] which sounds far from inspiring. Initially two pounds was paid on a boy's admission, a sizeable sum for most families, but this paid for the boy's apprenticeship when he left. The school was also unusual in that funding for the boys did not come from a common source; instead, boys wore badges on their famous blue coats noting their sponsors. This in turn meant that as rental incomes varied, so did the number of boys admitted and apprenticed. Samuel was at Queen Elizabeth Hospital from 1733-9 where his fees were paid by funds left by the school's founder, John Carr.

In its early years, the school had low educational standards. In November 1606 the boys were required to work each day to make them "better able to get their living".[24] From the 1650s the rules stated that boys had to be at least ten years old and, free of sickness and any deformity which would hinder them from becoming apprentices. So the school's remit was not to care for the poor and needy, but to empower young men of the city to improve themselves and to prevent them becoming a burden on the public purse. Boys had to be a son of a freeman of the city, i.e. who had been born, educated or purchased his freedom there. They also needed to be approved by the mayor and other officers. The boys were taught literacy and accountancy to prepare them for apprenticeship, most commonly to a merchant or for a career at sea. But most of their source books were the Bible or various classical texts, so an understanding of the classical world was widespread, and provided stories for ballads, fairground plays, puppet and automata shows which were attended by all levels of society. Many of the tales were morally improving, encouraging children to learn good behaviour and to become loyal, law-abiding citizens.

In 1700 responsibility for the thirty-six boys was transferred from the charity's treasurer to the schoolmaster, to whom they were "farmed" at the rate of nine pounds, three shillings and four pence per head. The master was not paid a salary and had to feed, clothe and educate them and pay the wages of three female servants. In addition, Edward Colston provided seventy pounds per year to support six boys and the master was also paid eight pounds per year to collect the various rents from properties to support the school.[25] Responsibility for the boys was taken seriously, as a council member visited the school weekly and an annual visit was made by the mayor and aldermen when a boy entertained them with an anthem, which had replaced the oration, suggesting their classical education was in decline. The singer and eight senior boys were each given a shilling, and cakes and fruit were distributed.[26]

It is unclear how successful the school became, as the rental income which was its main funding fluctuated, and Bristol Corporation (council) as the school's governors sometimes plundered its funds. Masters were later employed on an annual basis, an arrangement unlikely to attract the cream of the profession. Annual accounts were kept and signed off by the governors, but there were significant variations in the numbers of pupils charged for, not all of whom seem to have been recorded.

The ruinous school adjoining the chapel was rebuilt in 1706 to include a fine, classical- style stone house for the master which included a garden, a large schoolroom with dormitory above it, a play ground and an indoor space for recreation in bad weather. It was on the corners of Park, Unity and Denmark Streets, part of which is now a bank; the rest became the Society of Merchant Venturers' Technical College which was rebuilt c.1880. It is now — like many buildings in the city centre — expensive private flats.

2

SAMUEL

In November 1739, Samuel left his school to be apprenticed to Alderman Lyde, "an eminent Virginia Merchant"[1] as a scrivener. Thomas Chatterton, the famous fraud and poet, attended the much larger school, Colston's Hospital before training to be a clerk with a solicitor, which mostly involved copying out documents. This was such boring work that Chatterton trawled antiquarian booksellers and his local church's muniments room in search of old documents which inspired him to invent a mediaeval cleric whose alleged poetry was eventually exposed as fraudulent.

All businesses had to keep track of their accounts, maintain stock and journals and copy all letters before sending them. Training as a scrivener was thus a route for Samuel to learn his master's business, as well as practicing handwriting, and developing patience.

This author used to visit a local history group in south Bristol. One day a young boy was mentioned, and it was said that for some time he was taken in by various families; he ate with them, and slept in the same big bed as the families' own children, yet none of the group understood why as he was not related to any of them. A suggestion was made that his grandmother had died; others thought the father had been a soldier and mother a ballerina, so perhaps local people made their own arrangements to deal with single abandoned or orphaned children.

This taking in of children by neighbours probably explains why England and other Protestant countries did not create institutions for abandoned children as was common from the Middle Ages in Catholic countries, especially Italy and Spain.[2] Nor were there institutions for "fallen" women who became pregnant out of wedlock. Under Elizabethan Poor Laws, they were taken in by the parish where they were deemed to have "settlement". This was the parish where a person was born, but when a woman married this changed to the parish where husband had either been born or served his apprenticeship. The working poor could remain at home and their income supplemented with 'outdoor relief' to help them cope. But the destitute often ended up in the work house if able bodied or the poor house if elderly or infirm. Problems arose when couples came from distant parts in search of work. If a woman was widowed, she could be forced to move to her husband's home where she was a stranger but would be cared for by the overseers of the poor.

Such women were unlikely to find work again, as they would not be able to provide references from an employer, so for many, this was a lifetime of poverty or a death sentence. In the mid-eighteenth century, as the gentry became more mobile, attending various spas and London for 'the season', permanent work for servants became harder to find; some women were forced into prostitution, sometimes with unfortunate consequences. A source claimed this meant this prevented them from becoming good servants wives or prostitutes. Some young women, sent away from home to work at an early age, were ignorant of what was happening to their bodies. When they became pregnant, some tried to dispose of their newborns, but were generally found out and put on trial for infanticide. The fact that this illegal shows it was common enough to warrant action; it was hanging offence which shows how seriously it was taken. Some were raped by their employers who threw them out into the street when their condition became known.

Women were sometimes held solely responsible for becoming

pregnant, just as Eve was blamed for tempting Adam. In America, indentured servants were often raped by their masters, but as servants in general were considered to be depraved so rape was not a crime. The servant was often whipped, and fined for the time she took off work to care for any child she had. But as she probably had no money, the length of her servitude was extended. Her child would become a servant till adulthood, but given their poor living standards, this could be a life sentence.[3]

By the mid eighteenth century, England was beginning to replace the institutions destroyed by Henry VIII's Reformation. Many towns had lying-in hospitals for women to recover from childbirth, and dispensaries and infirmaries were founded. London's great hospitals such as Guy's, Westminster, St George's, Middlesex and Royal London were founded and the mediaeval St Thomas' re-founded, as charities. None of these were established by a monarch, though royalty and aristocrats often contributed generously to them.

England's first institution for orphans was the Foundling Hospital, founded by Captain Coram in London in the 1740s. But even this was not for orphans as we understand the term because children were often handed in by their mothers. Coram was a ship's captain and understood the problems of families left behind by sailors, who were often not paid until they returned, or were away so long that their family's resources were exhausted and the wives had to seek work which prevented them from caring for their children.

Sending children into service or apprenticeships in England meant that families were smaller than elsewhere, averaging only three or fewer children at home at one time. Such numbers suggest they were forebears of the modern nuclear family. An account of a British labourer in the late eighteenth century provides an image of how the long winter evenings were spent, with the woman spinning while the husband repaired shoes and played with the children, suggesting childcare was not entirely left to the mother.[4]

By contrast, in the American colonies, families were often large and healthy, especially in the northern, seafaring areas where they lived with plentiful clean air and healthy food and outdoor exercise. The practice of 'bundling', or pre-marital intimacy was widespread in the northern states. It was claimed to produce:

> "a long-jawed, raw-boned hardy race of whoreson whalers, wood-cutters, fishermen and peddlers and strapping corn-fed wenches, who by their united efforts tended marvellously towards populating these notable parts of the country called Nantucket, Piscatawny and Cape Cod".[5]

Gist's eldest daughter Mary married Virginian William Anderson who was the eldest of eleven children, and also had many cousins. Yet neither they, nor her sister Elizabeth and husband William Fowkes had any children. Samuel's master John Smith and his wife Mary had only two sons, John jun. and Joseph. When Smith died, Gist married Mary Smith and became the boys' guardian before the couple had two daughters, Mary and Elizabeth. Samuel amassed much wealth throughout his long lifetime, which would have passed on to a male heir, but after Mary died, he did not remarry.

Women far outnumbered men at the time due to the many men lost at sea and in wars, so Gist would have been spoilt for choice had he wished for female companionship. Widowers often struggled to manage their households; they sometimes married their house-keepers to make their presence under the same roof respectable. But Gist seems to have been content as a single man on his return to England, spending much of his time on the Exchange with his colleagues and rivals. Or perhaps he was focusing on amassing his fortune and did not want a wife or her relatives to inherit any of it.

❧

Samuel was taught literacy and numeracy at Queen Elizabeth's Hospital. The other Bristol charity school for boys, Bristol Grammar included teaching of the classics and of oratory, so Queen Elizabeth

Hospital probably did likewise. We have no details of young Samuel's schooldays, but school records note that some boys ran away or were forced to leave due to misdemeanours, such as one for theft in 1744, though strangely the boy was provided with new clothes on his departure.[6] But the school's income varied from year to year, and masters were employed on an annual basis, which suggests standards were not high.

Despite rising numbers of donations to the school in the early century, in 1739 there were still only thirty-six boys while Colston's Hospital had one hundred.[7] Dr Barratt's history of the city was written in 1789 and praised the city corporation in its care for the school but condemned the "narrow, selfish, factious spirit of others". This comment is opaque at this distance. Bristol-born but London-educated and resident Edward Colston, was prevented from making a generous donation to support several boys there. He had long been absent from the city and had retired to a modest residence at Mortlake, near London, so he may also have been resented for no longer being a local man. Or it may have reflected the merchant's strict adherence to High Church principles, refusing to support the sons of non-Anglicans, a problem which has plagued his trustees ever since. The boys lived and were educated in a fine school building which was erected in 1706, and included a large school-room and dormitory above, and indoor and outdoor play areas. Beyond the front door was the large open space of College Green. So it seems the young Samuel had a better start in life than most boys of his age.

Only healthy, able-bodied boys were accepted into the school, to justify the investment in their future, so Samuel must have been well cared for before his admission. Many people claim that the concept of childhood didn't exist at the time, but children did play, as shown by several paintings by Hogarth, though he showed them with large heads and dressed as adults, and these were from families rich enough to commission such art. Some boys were apprenticed as children, which meant they qualified in a trade in their early teens but when they qualified, they were not strong enough to work as adults or to become freemen and run their own businesses. This is

why, even after compulsory education was introduced in the mid -
nineteenth century, streets were still so full of children. Many boys
were in a form of limbo, employed to run errands or make small
deliveries.

§&.

On 22 November 1739 young Samuel's apprenticeship as a
scrivener began with Lyonel Lyde Esquire, presumably for the usual
seven years. The necessary eight pounds was paid from the school
founder, John Carr's charity which had paid Samuel's education.[8]
Thus it is unclear how or exactly when he was sent to Lyde's agent
in Virginia, John Smith. An apprenticeship was a legal contract by
which the master undertook to train the boy, provide food clothing
and lodging with his family and ensure the boy attended divine
service each Sunday. In return, the apprentice had to obey his
master and was forbidden from leaving or marrying during his
term. The master became his legal guardian, so had a duty of care
and the right to discipline the boy when necessary, though the defin-
ition was not clear and could be open to abuse. Newspapers sometimes carried notices from masters seeking runaway apprentices and
servants. Sometimes such servants were noted as being black, so it
could be unclear if they were slaves or indentured servants.

   This Lyde was a merchant who was Bristol's sheriff in 1722,
mayor in 1735 and Master of the Merchant Venturers in 1741, so
he was a man of substance involved in international trade. This
apprenticeship, by the end of which he became a merchant, was the
grounds for Samuel becoming a freeman of the city on 2 November
1752.

   But Samuel was sent to the colonies, the conditions under which
are unclear. He was not listed as a servant or apprentice to the plantations. No mention was made of any time limit on his indenture,
which has also left no trace, even though it should have been
recorded and a copy left with Bristol Corporation at their *Tolzey* or
council house on Corn Street. Thus, it is unclear who was ultimately
responsible for his welfare and training. Perhaps the Virginia

merchants had some system of private agreements which were supervised and policed amongst themselves, akin to the ancient guilds. Or it could point to something far more sinister.

Latimer's Annals of Bristol provides an extraordinary record of the abuses in Bristol, which were probably echoed in every major port in Britain, indicating how widespread this abuse had become by 1654.

"A remarkable corporate ordinance was adopted on September 29th. It premises that many complaints had been made of the inveigling, purloining, and stealing away boys, maids and others, and transporting them beyond the seas, and there disposing of them for private gin, without the knowledge of their parents and friends. 'This being a crime of much villainy,' it was ordered that all boys, maids, and others thenceforth transported as servants should before shipment have their indentures of service enrolled in the Tolzey Book. A penalty of twenty pounds was imposed on any ship captain or officer receiving persons not so enrolled, and the Water-bailiff was directed to use due diligence in searching ships for those designed to be carried off. Copies of the ordinance were ordered to be posted up in convenient places that none might plead ignorance. The offence was, however, too profitable to be suppressed by a mere by-law, and it is certain that kidnapping was habitually encouraged by many merchants throughout the century, and was not uncommon even later. On September 1655, two men, convicted of "man stealing" were condemned by the magistrates to stand one hour in the pillory on three market days, with the offence placarded on their breasts. If the sentence had ended here, the wrath of the populace would have inflicted such a vengeance on the malefactors as would have made a lasting impression on all engaged in the infamous pursuit. But the merchants, sitting as magistrates, with a tender regard for mercantile interests, ordered that the villains should be 'protected', that is guarded from the missiles of spectators — so that the punishment was little more than formal. In august 1656, a man was committed for trial 'for spiriting away two boys'. In 1661 another wretch, who had robbed a boy of money on the highway and then stolen the lad himself, 'being known to be a common man stealer, and spirit that enticeth away people', was also committed for trial; but as the Sessions record is lost, the fate of both these men is unknown. A little later, another knave was ordered "to stand in the pillory at the High Cross next market day for half an hour, with an inscription on his breast of his offence —kidnapping. To be protected. The frivolous punishments inflicted on offenders by a bench which evidently sympathised with them, of course had no deterring effect on a profitable traffic. In July 1662, the Corporation representing the trading class as well as merchants, petitioned the King for power to examine the masters and passengers on board ships bound to the plantations with a view to prevent the "spiriting away" of unwary persons by manstealers, and the escape of rogues and apprentices — an ordinance of 1654. The King's response is not preserved, but the traffic had already attracted the attention of the Privy Council. In July 1660, the minute book states that their lordships had received information that children were being daily enticed away from their parents and servants from their masters, being caught up by merchants and ship captains trading to Virginia and the West Indies and there sold as merchandise; moreover that if such kidnapped people were found in a ship before her departure, the captain would not liberate them without he received compensation —" barbarous, inhumane thing". From the order which follows of the searching of three ships then in the Thames, and the rescue of the children they contained, the system appears to have been as common in London as in Bristol".[9]

Punishment in the pillory is generally considered to have been a form of shaming; it is alleged that the crowd threw flowers at Defoe when he was forced to stand there. But this is to seriously underestimate the punishment. Pillories were in the market place, and were used on market days when crowds gathered, with plentiful vegetable and animal waste to use as missiles to express their displeasure. Whole cabbages and turnips could be hurled at felons whose heads were fixed, preventing them from getting out of the way; the punishment could cause severe head injuries, even death. Hence there are cases on record where offenders wore protective hats, or where they had to be rescued from the market mob.

In Bristol in the early eighteenth century, those sentenced to the pillory were subjected to such violence that they hired ruffians to protect them. There were accounts of riots breaking out between the two groups. A forger was sentenced to a year in jail, a heavy fine, and to stand in the pillory for two days, on the last of which "he was severely pelted with eggs by a common mob" who had fought their way past his defenders.[10] A more extreme case from some years later for a man sentenced for a "filthy offence" he "hired a hundred colliers to protect him, and provided himself with an iron skull cap, and thickly covered his body with brown paper."[11] This unnamed offence was probably of a sexual nature, as homosexuality was vigorously punished in the city at the time.

Samuel's role seems to have been more that of the child of a merchant, sent to learn the local practices and conditions. He was described as a 'shop boy', suggesting he swept up, ran errands etc., but his education would have been wasted in this role, and nobody would have paid for his passage to carry out such menial tasks. Such work would have been given to a slave: either too young or too old and infirm for field work. But this still does not exclude the possibility he had been transported against his will, as slaves could better themselves by learning skills and earning money, and some eventually purchased their own freedom.

Gist was probably trained in keeping records, accounts and copying letters and agreements to customers and suppliers which allowed him to build up a good working knowledge of the business. His relationship with Lyde suggests the trade with John Smith's shop grew during his employment, in both the amount and variety of goods imported, in parallel with the increased amount of tobacco shipped from Hanover Town as the settlement flourished. The tobacco crop was shipped in autumn, so orders for goods to be brought on return trips had to be placed with the relevant merchants in England well in advance, and space on ships allocated for it. In 1773, his business partner Zachariah Clarke advertised the dissolution of his business, requesting all debts be paid immediately. He offered a "genteel assortment of goods" for sale at discounts, suggesting there was a significant middle class who followed English fashions.[12] But fashions often changed between a colonial order being placed and the arriving, so though profitable, such a market was high risk, and goods could not be returned if they were deemed unsuitable when they arrived.

If Samuel had remained in Bristol, he probably would have been apprenticed into some local trade and kept in touch with his school friends and surviving relatives. But he was unusual in being sent — perhaps against his will — on a dangerous sea journey to live with strangers in a strange land. This must have strained his already robust capacity to survive. It must have been lonely for him, at least at first. Or given his vulnerability and lack of options, he may have adapted and seen it as a grand adventure, a new world to be explored. Whatever the conditions of his arrival in Virginia, he seems to have thrived, though this may have taken some time. He outlived most of his peers and when he at last died, left huge legacies on both sides of the Atlantic.

3

VIRGINIA

Before modern policing was established in nineteenth century Europe, brutal punishments — now referred to as mediaeval — had long been used to discourage criminal behaviour. Even the horrors of being hung, drawn and quartered were justified as death alone was not considered a sufficient punishment. Everyone died. Life was seen as transitory, so punishment required true suffering, and the public needed to witness it as a warning should they feel tempted to commit crime.

In the early eighteenth century, communal land and public forests were increasingly enclosed, especially in London's hinterland, which deprived local people of foraging, grazing and building materials. When locals fought back by breaking down fences and killing deer, the first Prime Minister Robert Walpole passed a series of Black Acts which turned what had been minor misdemeanours into capital offences. Many of these were commuted to transportation, and the practice of shipping felons to the Americas became a profitable business for several Bristol merchants including the Lyde family. They were paid to ship felons as ballast on the way out, though they sometimes had to wait for the courts, so they did not always arrive in time to return with the autumn harvest of tobacco.

From 1718 the government authorised transportation as a form of punishment, and ports like Bristol made full use of this. During war time, these prisoners were even expected to fight alongside regular soldiers.[1] In 1726 the keeper of the city's Newgate jail requested payment from the city corporation for transporting "sundry prisoners to distant places out of the common way".[2] So this became an updated version of the ancient punishment of banishment. Before this time, the friends and family of the condemned could occasionally obtain reprieves.

Europe has a long history of emigration, but it is in these British Isles that it has come to define the nation as a whole, with people continuing to leave their homeland for pastures new. The practice can be dated back to the Middle Ages, when life for many became a living hell, when Europe was beset with floods, droughts, storms, famines and plagues over many decades in the thirteenth and fourteenth centuries.[3] The collapse of the population affected everyone from the poorest up to the rulers; civic authority declined as the hungry and unemployed took to crime. People in the countryside retreated to walled towns for safety, but these became crowded and filthy, creating a perfect environment for plagues and epidemics, especially the Black Death, which wiped out an estimated third of Europe's population. England was further ravaged by the Wars of the Roses, a series of battles of unprecedented savagery over decades and which depopulated large areas of the north. Peace came with the coronation of Henry VII, so the savagery was still of recent memory and served as a warning to his son Henry VIII of the necessity to ensure the stability of the crown and pass it on to a strong male heir.

No amount of prayer, fasting or penance brought people relief from their suffering. Many came to believe that God had abandoned them, so they turned to material rather than spiritual comfort. Clerics were often illiterate, poorly paid and/or corrupt, so provided poor leadership when their flock sought reasons for their sufferings, they would scapegoat outsiders such as Jews and witches. The real culprit was probably a prolonged ice age which struck northern Europe and lingered into Tudor times as can be seen in the heavy clothing worn by people in contemporary paintings by Brugel. The prolonged cold hampered agriculture, so people relied more heavily on seafood, and were forced to travel further to find it, resulting in some reaching North America. It may also explain why the Georgians ate such huge quantities of meat rather than grains, which, combined with the preference for alcoholic drinks over water, made gout become such a common complaint, especially among the better off.

But this prolonged storm of misery eventually provided a rainbow with a pot of gold at its end. Survivors produced an unprecedented outpouring of scientific discoveries as their focus shifted from faith to science for explanations of their suffering. Europeans invented guns, clockwork, eyeglasses, crossbows, compasses and the printing press, the last of which helped accelerate improvements in technology and the exchange and spread of knowledge.[4] As a result, Europe in the following centuries not only recovered from its time of darkness, but paved the way for the Enlightenment and the Industrial Revolution, and so the modern world. This also provided survivors with dreams of a better future and the means to achieve it. Instead of a heavenly paradise, they sought paradise on earth. Before the discovery of the New World, the only way to heaven was to lead a good, Christian life and then to die. But when Columbus returned and published his discoveries, the ports of Spain were flooded with hopeful emigrants, believing they could reach paradise by sailing there in a boat.

But the New World was not paradise; nor was it a blank canvas on which Europeans could project their fantasies of a life of leisure. The huge tracts of land claimed by early aristocrats had to be worked, and indigenous people refused to become their servants.

Life for the poor in England had been grim since Henry VIII closed the monasteries which had provided a safety net to care for the sick, infirm and disabled. The religious houses had been celibate communities which kept a lid on the population, where the sons of the rich could enter, to be kept in reserve should the family line die out. But the Tudors failed to take on the many roles of the churches, so the population exploded. Towns and cities from the sixteenth century onwards struggled to cope with their soaring populations, especially among the lower classes.

Under Elizabeth, a range of laws were passed to punish vagrants by incarcerating them in workhouses. Or return them to their places of birth. Wealthy benefactors provided legacies to found and fund charity schools to train young boys to support their family by learning a trade. Almshouses for the aged were also founded, especially in major port cities for ancient mariners and their widows. Donations were also made to pay for the young to be apprenticed, to learn a trade and be able to support themselves and their families, and for dowries to help young girls make successful marriages. Many young boys in ports like Bristol were trained to become merchants or mariners.

Henry VIII sold off the treasures of the monasteries and much of their property, but by the end of his reign, England was already bankrupt. The Spanish found gold — and even more, silver — in the New World. The English were late arrivals to the Americas, so were beaten to the precious metals by the Catholic nations. The most famous early English immigrants were driven by a desire for religious freedom, as Andrew Marvell wrote, to escape from "prelate's rage" when James I and Archbishop Laud declared there was only one religion in England, and it was of the Church of England. In New England the settlers aimed to follow the Geneva model, by establishing a Kingdom of God in the wilderness, whilst other northern colonies believed in religious tolerance for all.[5] The religious schism that tore apart old England under Cromwell had done the same in New England from 1635.

The earliest English settlers preceded these disputes, with the first settlement at Jamestown in 1607, and like Maryland, it was tolerant towards religion. In Virginia, huge tracts of land granted to aristocrats were intended to be worked by indentured servants. When the monasteries were closed and the land sold off, more people wished to own land, for a chance to better themselves. Some early settlers were educated men, so one of their first acts was to found a university and they soon became self governing, echoing the practice of local government by justices of the peace in England.

Spain and Portugal used slaves in South America, especially indigenous people in the silver mines of Potosi, but also Africans. Following the Black Death, the Pope had permitted enslavement of non-Christians to cope with the resulting manpower shortage. But it was initially rejected by the English as a foreign, Catholic practice, which was offensive to their proud tradition of independence. Their Reformation had been based on becoming free of the Church of Rome which had authorised such enslavement. The first Africans arrived in North America in 1609, but they were treated as servants and allocated land at the end of their agreed term. Black and white servants were initially treated equally.

From the early seventeenth century poor people signed contracts with ships' captains to transport them to new lives in the colonies; they were sold as indentured servants, and forced to work for their master to pay off their passage. Some were lured on board ships with the promise of a set of clothes or of land, tools and corn to set up as farmers at the end of their contracts, usually between four and seven years. But few agreements were honoured; not many servants survived, and the fortunate few who were granted land found it deep in Indian Territory.[6] As news of conditions spread, the supply of free servants dried up.

In 1690 a John Lyme complained to a Maryland court that he had been given a four year indenture on board ship, and that witnesses could prove this, but the document had been taken. Claims were made that thousands of white children were taken before the Virginian courts to be sentenced to periods of slavery based on their ages. Initially, if under twenty years old, they had to serve four years to pay back their passage to the colony. This changed to a graded system; those aged twelve to twenty served five years, and those under twelve had to serve till they were adults, reflecting the amount of work the young people and even infants were capable of achieving. In March 1655 Virginia passed the first law to discriminate between servants by making Irish servants serve for longer, and for years to be added to their existing contracts.[7]

Thousands of children were rounded up each year from the streets of major towns and cities, especially London, to be sent to the colonies as so-called apprentices. But they were trained in little more than hard work and abuse. John Donne (1571-1631), when dean at Westminster claimed that the removal of vagrant children from the streets cleansed the capital and had already made it the envy of England's enemies.[8] But Donne was not an impartial commentator. He was closely linked with many members of the Virginia Company and for a time considered emigrating to become their official recorder there. In his poetry he compared lands as seductive women, a concept pushing the limits of acceptability in England's reformed church and would today get him trolled within an inch of his life.

> *"Licence my roaving hands, and let them go,*
> *Before, behind, between above, below."*[9]

In 1678 James I became concerned about the many idle young people infesting the streets, so urged Sir Thomas Smythe, governor of the East India Company, to send them to Virginia, claiming this would be a "deed of charity" as an alternative to an "idle life of vagabonds".[10]

Complaints were made when this abuse of children was discovered, but it was countered with the claim that a new life in the colonies was for their benefit, so the Virginia Company's kidnapping continued. If any children misbehaved, the company could punish them and "dispose of any of those children... as cause shall require",[11] a phrase that allows a terrifying range of interpretations.

The company targeted healthy young people from their teens to their late twenties, who would survive the rough passage and endure the hard work and heat. But objections began to be raised when children of respectable citizens were taken. In 1670 it became a crime, punishable by death, but this was never applied, so had little or no impact. It was never a high priority for the government, especially as the children were often held in crime-ridden slum areas where officers feared for their lives. The term kidnapping is made up of the slang word to nab, a kid or child. The first citation of it in the Oxford English Dictionary dates from 1682 in reference to a boy being rescued from a man intent on sending him to Jamaica. The trade was forced underground to become a form of organised crime. Those heinous criminals were called *spirits*, who *spirited away* their victims. London's criminal net was wide. In 1767 the deputy Overseer of the workhouse in Oxford was taken before London's Lord Mayor for having lured an eighteen-year-old girl in his care to London where he had tried to sell her to be sent abroad.[12]

But this practice had a surprising precedent. In a recent BBC4 documentary, Abducted: Elizabeth I's Child Actors, Katherine Rundel described the kidnapping in 1600 of thirteen-year-old Thomas Clifton from a London street. He was taken by the manager of the elite Blackfriar's Theatre, but when his father tried to retrieve him, it appeared that Henry Evans had acted under a royal warrant. His partner was the singing master for the Chapel Royal, who was allowed by Elizabeth I to steal children to become choristers. Young Clifton was returned to his family the following day but not on the grounds that the kidnapping was illegal, but that he was not to become a chorister.

In the wake of Cromwell's invasion, children were sent from Ireland to New England and Virginia from 1653. A thousand each of girls and boys were sent to Jamaica in 1655. In September 1654 Bristol Corporation passed an extraordinary ordinance in response to many complaints made of the

"inveigling, purloining and stealing away of boys, maids and others, transporting them beyond the seas and there disposing of them for private gain, without the knowledge of their parents and friends."

From this date, all servants to be shipped to the colonies were to have their indentures of service enrolled at the Tolzey or pay a fine of twenty pounds.[13] These records can be consulted at the Bristol Record Office, but Gist is not listed.

Throughout the eighteenth and nineteenth centuries in England, parishes advertised children to be apprenticed, sometimes describing them as plump to show they were well fed so probably robust, and a worthwhile investment. It seems there was never any follow up, so once the children were passed to a master, their fate was with God rather than the authorities. The poet John Day, friend of several of Birmingham's Lunar Men had struggled to find a suitable wife, as he sought a woman who was his intellectual equal, but who would be submissive to him, an unlikely combination. He obtained two girls from workhouses in the hope of training them so he could choose the most suitable to become his wife. This stretched the notion of training into the realms of sexual abuse and exploitation by a respected — if eccentric — member of the gentry.

And yet in September 1833 Bristol's Corporation of the Poor planned to send seventy boys and girls, some as young as twelve, and some entire families, to Van Diemen's Land, now Tasmania in Australia. This prison was established for the most hardened offenders from Botany Bay. But all of this group were deemed to have agreed of their own free will, and on arrival to work for three years, again as so-called apprentices. It seems the only doubts raised were whether local poor rates should be used beyond the limits of the British Dominions.[14]

Why did the exportation of the poor continue in Britain for so long? Cecil Rhodes (1853–1902) was the arch-imperialist, and is now demonised as a promoter of white settlement in Africa. When he addressed an angry group of unemployed men in London's East End, he claimed that Imperialism was:

"a solution for the social problems ... in order to save the forty million inhabitants of the United Kingdom from bloody civil war, we colonial statesmen must acquire new lands to settle the surplus population, to provide new markets for the goods provided in the factories and mines."

He summed up his views with the extraordinary claim:

"if you want to avoid civil war, you must become imperialists".[15]

This shines a new light on British history. At the end of the eighteenth-century, when France was in turmoil, Britain came terrifyingly close to following her. Some sources claim there were as many men in uniform keeping the peace at home as there were fighting on the continent. There were further disturbances over food shortages when peace came, and again in the 1840s, known as the Hungry Forties in Britain, on the continent it was another violent period. The rise of evangelism, in particular, the work of the Wesleys amongst the poor is often credited with averting civil war. But Rhodes' claim seems more likely. By exporting her poor and her troublemakers — who were often seen as the same — to the colonies, Britain exported the dangers of rebellion at home. This is also echoed in the rise of Nazism, which was fuelled by a need for lebensraum, or living space. Many German states also dumped their criminals in North America.

John Esquemeling wrote in 1684 of how West Indian planters traded servants like horses at fairs. Some even went to Europe and England to lure young men from towns and cities to the colonies where they were forced to work harder than African slaves. He claimed they were poorly fed and clothed, and that he had witnessed them being beaten to death by their masters. These young Europeans were said to suffer an illness known as a coma, the complete loss of their senses which was attributed to the change of climate: "persons of good quality and tender education" were said to be more commonly afflicted.[16]

The production of tobacco in Virginia was massively labour-intensive; the plants required constant weeding and pest control. Where
the soil was heavy, it had to be broken up around the plants, and in
low-lying areas such as the Tidewater where Samuel lived, the
plants were grown in raised beds to prevent their roots rotting. The
earliest settlers had been granted huge estates in return for
importing servants, which fuelled the emptying of English streets
and jails. In the 1630s a new, ruthless breed of planters arrived who
caused a massive rise in output from four hundred pounds per
worker in the 1620s to a thousand by the end of the century. No
improvements in technology were involved, so the workers must
have been driven beyond exhaustion, many of them to an early
grave, which paved the way for the brutal treatment of African
slaves.[17]

The English Civil War (1642–51) caused a fall in birth rates, so
by the Restoration of the Monarchy in 1660 there were fewer
people to become servants for the plantations. The war also
changed the type of immigrants arriving. Cromwell used the
colonies as a dumping ground for the poor, including the Irish, but
also for his opponents the Royalists, who were unlikely to accept or
adapt to a life of servitude. The situation was worsened after the
Restoration when members of Cromwell's New Model Army were
sent to the colonies, where they became involved in every rebellion
which followed. This caused increasing opposition to the shipping
of prisoners of war and criminals, as they brought more problems
than benefits.

By the 1660s the brutal treatment of servants — which involved
assaults, rape and murder — became so infamous that the supply of
people dried up. To try to remedy the situation, in 1662 the House
of Burgesses in Virginia ordered masters to provide adequate provi-
sions and clothing, and to moderate the punishment of their
servants, who were even given the right to complain, though this
had little impact.[18] But as the planters were also the justices, they
were never going to punish themselves or their neighbours.

The situation worsened when the Great Plague caused another collapse of the population, and the Great Fire of London created a building boom in the capital which drew tradesmen from across the land, delaying the post-war recovery and rebuilding in the rest of the country. This led to a shortage of servants to emigrate, and those who did go were of lower quality. The situation was not helped by the planters, as in 1663 Maryland rescinded the promise of land at the end of the term of servitude, with masters only providing clothes, tools and corn.[19] It seems "Chesapeake planters did not abandon indentured servitude; it abandoned them".[20] The planters, like the first settlers, assumed that the supply was limitless. At the Restoration of the Monarchy in 1660, King Charles II was in need of money so he sold a number of trade monopolies, one of which was the Royal African Company. Initially its interest was mainly in gold but it began to ship slaves to the colonies in 1674.

Conditions were changing for Africans in North America, as in 1662 their status came to be defined by that of their mother,[21] suggesting many masters were raping their female slaves and refusing to recognise the children as their own. In 1667 a statute was passed which stated that baptism did not affect the state of bondage or freedom of a person,[22] which seems like more of the same. By this date, there were two groups of enslaved Africans arriving in North America. Those who came via the West Indies arrived in small numbers and were accustomed to the European system of servitude. Some arrived as free persons, with skills in demand who could own property at the end of their term in the same way as Europeans. This was possible, as before the 1660s there were only a few hundred Africans in Chesapeake.[23] But from the 1740s some were listed as serving for the term of their natural life, but this may have been due to them being deemed criminals, possibly for rebelling against their conditions. In the 1660s and '70s laws were passed to protect property rather than to punish Africans.[24]

But as the numbers of slaves increased, they increasingly came directly from Africa rather than via the West Indies. This was probably via their own ships to avoid the naked Navigation Acts, but also to prevent their ships being attacked by Caribbean torpedo worms.

The slaves were thus more 'African', i.e. they had not learned British language and behaviour, so were less likely to accept their status as slaves. This situation led to discriminatory laws such as Virginia's first 'Black Code' with a statute to prevent 'negro insurrections'. By 1691 runaway slaves were to be pursued by a group, so his private property was defended by the state.[25] By 1705 Virginia had become a 'chattel slave society' wherein ownership was enshrined in law.

The Royal Africa Company's monopoly ended in 1698, opening up the slave trade to merchants from ports such as Bristol and even Aberdeen. Unlike normal shipping, huge investment was required to fit out ships with shackles, extra food and water etc, and to provide goods to trade with African leaders, so slave ships tended to be larger than normal. The voyages could last up to two years, and there were many risks along the way, such as the unsuitability of trade goods, the lack of slaves, their rebellion and outbreaks of illness en route, storms and pirates. Plenty of people were still willing to invest, and could wait for returns which could be huge. By the end of the eighteenth century, slaves were arriving in Chesapeake at the rate of about a thousand per year. By 1708 the population of the area consisted of twelve thousand black people and eighteen thousand white people.

The tipping point came with Bacon's Rebellion, led by Nathaniel Bacon in 1676. He was a descendant of James I's Lord Chancellor and related to Governor Berkeley, so was close to the ruling elite, and his rebellion had huge consequences. It began when his farm was attacked by local Indians and he declared war on them but the Governor wished to appease them to help in his battle with the French. Bacon drew support from all classes below the government, rather than the usual lower class rabble. By this time, there were growing calls for reform as many free settlers were struggling against unfair taxes, which prevented freed servants from obtaining or holding onto the land they were entitled to. Bacon almost led to the colony declaring its independence a century before this was eventually achieved.

The uprising collapsed when Bacon suddenly died of dysentery, and his supporters were brutally punished. But he had highlighted a problem that had been simmering in American and Caribbean colonies for some time: the lack of a middle class as defence against uprisings and invasions.

Before the establishment of police forces in the early nineteenth century law was enforced in Britain by justices of the peace, magistrates, parish constables and community intervention. When serious disturbances occurred, most areas had a sizeable middle class of tradesmen and small landowners who were bound by honour and self-interest to intervene. If a gentleman saw a robbery on the highway, he was expected to defend the victim, and summon help to arrest the offender. Newspapers sometimes published condemnations of men who failed to do so. This system seems to have broken down in Britain due to the rise in the number of absentee landlords, who preferred to spend their time in London or the various spas rather than serving the local community whose rents allowed them such luxury. One reason for the introduction of fox hunting in England was that it encouraged the wealthy to spend more time at their estates and to engage with their local communities.

In the West Indies, planters were encouraged to breed with slaves to produce an intermediary yeoman class, which was made necessary by the climate which killed so many Europeans, preventing them from filling the void. The mixing of races was condemned in North America, where the solution became the creation of a white middle class, which involved separating European from African workers.

Up to this point, both groups of servants had worked together and been housed, fed and treated equally. After Bacon's Rebellion, the races were increasingly housed and fed differently, and whites acquired rights while blacks were systematically treated worse.[26] This was the start of the practice of segregation based on perceived racial superiority.

Yet England continued to send its criminals to America. Judge Jeffreys became infamous for his 'bloody assizes' when he ordered the execution and transportation of most of those involved in the Monmouth Uprising of 1685. During the trials he heard a boy had been taken from prison and transported. Many local jailers supplemented their meagre civic wages by selling convicts facing death sentences to be sent to the New World slave markets. Jeffreys uncovered the scheme and the widespread corruption in many ports. Bristol's mayor was fined a massive one thousand pounds for his involvement.[27]

Like his patron/employer Lionel Lyde, Gist's surname is a rare one. Lyde was a prominent Virginia merchant. By the early eighteenth century in Bristol; he worked with Quakers including the ship owner and slave trader Isaac Hobhouse, which suggests he may have been a member of the group. In the seventeenth century, in Bristol and London, many groups such as Puritans, then Quakers, who were excluded from public life by the Anglican establishment, became active trading in tobacco and iron, settling mostly in King William County, Virginia. A ship owned by Lyonel Lyde, the Anna Maria, was sized by the Spanish in 1724 when returning from Jamaica to Bristol. It was eventually recovered with the help of the South Sea Company.[28] But if Lyde had been a member of one of these groups, he would not have been able to hold public office as alderman and mayor. In 1721 he became involved in an iron furnace in Virginia with John and Walter King whose surname suggests they were Catholics, so another marginalised group. In the national archives are claims for compensation submitted by merchants who lost money during the War of Independence; these include Gist and also Walter King, formerly of Virginia, who is recorded as owning considerable land in the backcountry, and having a tenant and agents there.[29]

The following year they took on a property on the north side of the Rappahannock River where they carried out mining with indentured servants for about eight years. In 1725, twenty-four people were put on board a frigate in Bristol, bound as servants for only four years, which suggests they were skilled tradesmen who could speedily earn the money to pay for their passage, so they were probably ironworkers. The iron was sent to London Liverpool and Bristol, suggesting they were the home ports of the other partners.

In 1703 Jamaica waived port dues if a ship brought sufficient white servants. In 1729 Isaac Hobhouse shipped thirteen "servants" from London to the island of Jamaica.[30] They were often lured on board ship by the promise of a set of clothes. On arrival they were sold by the ships' captains to the highest bidder. Destitute parents were sometimes forced to sell their children to save themselves from being sold. This trade in human flesh flourished in Bristol. In 1703 it was claimed people were sold in Jamaica for fourteen to eighteen pounds; once there, the servants were forced to earn their freedom by working for their masters for four years if an adult, and seven if a child. These servants were often kept in the Bridewell prison till the ship sailed, so they were treated as convicts, but unlike criminals, their term was not legally fixed; if they angered their masters in any way, their term of indenture could be extended. In 1729 a young man was forced onto a ship by relatives who wished to claim his inheritance of eight hundred pounds.[31]

In 1721 Lyde and seven other Bristolians were involved in a Virginian ironworks and the provision of slaves to work it. Lyde also transported felons to Virginia and Maryland and invested in glassworks,[32] probably producing bottles to transport Hotwell water to the West Indies as a treatment for tropical illnesses. In 1745 this same Alderman Lyde applied to Bristol Corporation to be paid three guineas for transporting eight convicts to Virginia. But he left four women behind as they were less suited to heavy work.[33]

The British criminal justice system was being hijacked, no longer to rid the streets of the poor, but to provide labour in the American colonies, and to subsidise Atlantic shipping. This meant that transportation for a criminal was only an option if they would sell for high prices in the colonies, so justices no longer made any attempt to link punishment to the crimes committed. It also deprived Britain of large numbers of able-bodied men, so the proportion of people in need, such as the many single women, the elderly and disabled increased. This further exacerbated the huge loss of manpower at sea and during wartime.

In 1727 a Bristol ship The Castle purchased slaves at Andony, now modern Nigeria, paid for in part with iron and copper.[34] This shows how the infamous triangular trade evolved to include manufactured goods traded for slaves in Africa who were then sent to the West Indies and sold for sugar and tobacco. Eighteenth century Virginian newspapers sometimes advertised plantations for sale which could produce corn for export to the West Indies as the limited acreage of the islands led to them concentrating on exotic, high profit exports. They had to import basics such as food, often from North America: even from the northern colonies which were less supportive of slavery.

Iron and copper smelting began in the Bristol area when blacksmith Abraham Darby blacksmith was allowed to become a freeman of the city in 1707 without paying a fee as his skills were of benefit to the city. With three fellow Quakers, he established brass and iron foundries on the outskirts of the city. But it took him some time and industrial espionage to develop improved methods of iron working, which he patented. This made smelting cheaper, lowering the price of cooking pots for the poor and for the slave plantations. But when he failed to find investment to expand his business, in 1709 he moved to Coalbrookdale which became a leading centre for ironworking, with its famous iron bridge. Smelting works continued at Baptist Mills and Crews Hole on the outskirts of Bristol, still run mostly by Quakers, where they produced copper cooking pans for sugar boiling and — most importantly but less famously — copper to plate the bottoms of ships to prevent the Caribbean toredo worms eating through their hulls. Copper barrels were often used to protect gunpowder from water damage, and from open flames.

In the early decades of the eighteenth century, ironworks developed in New England and Mr William Donne of Bristol, who owned two furnaces in Virginia, complained with other Bristol ironmongers to the House of Commons about the New England trade undercutting English wares. By 1738 the Bristol iron works were in decline, so the owners attempted, but failed, to ban the import of American iron. Some landlords in Gloucestershire raised concerns that American imports of iron would make wood on their lands useless and that local people would become impoverished.[35] This echoed the earlier battles between tobacco growers on both sides of the Atlantic.

⚜

But if Samuel was born an orphan, and sent abroad as a pauper, how did he achieve so much in such a short time? In 1735 this same Lyonel Lyde's son also left Queen Elizabeth's Hospital for an apprenticeship paid for by school funds. He was passed into the care of Joseph Ludlow, a ship's captain, and the school's records state "to go to Virginia".

Thus, young Lyde's and Gist's indentures raise a number of questions. Why was the son of an alderman and sometime mayor — one of the richest men in the city —being educated at a charity school? Why were his indentures also paid from public funds? And why was the younger Lyde — like the orphan Samuel — apparently sent abroad in the company of strangers?

Ludlow probably owned at least part of his vessel, with other investors to share the risk. But ships to the colonies at the time were mostly involved in importing colonial produce, which meant the ships often left England in ballast, which is why the transportation of emigrants, servants, convicts and slaves became so popular. John Dyer, brother of the Bristol diarist William was born c.1733. But when he died his eldest son Samuel, born in 1756, was sent to Colston's Hospital school. He was then apprenticed to a merchant in Virginia where he continued long enough to be remembered in his uncle's will of 1797.[36] Thus the practice of foreign apprenticeships from Bristol charity schools, which was the making of Gist, was apparently common practice and continued for several decades more.

Apprenticeships differed from agreements made by servants. They were often overseen by trade guilds to ensure high standards of training, that the secrets of their trade were kept, and that all trade was honest. Bristol was a popular city for apprentices; young men were recorded as coming from thirty counties to train there. But conditions varied widely. If the master was rich and generous, the apprentice would be well fed and clothed, so his lifestyle — though it could involve long hours and hard work — could be much better than at home.[37] The apprenticeships were generally signed by the boy's parents, but the mayor was legally responsible for orphans, and as a member of Bristol Corporation, was also a governor of the Queen Elizabeth's Hospital, so he must have arranged for young Gist's training. Bristol's mayor in 1739 was a tobacconist, Stephen Clutterbuck, so he probably sold the Virginian tobacco that Lyde imported. As Samuel's master, Lyde acted in the stead of a parent to the orphan, and his close business ties should have ensured the boy was well cared for once he set sail for Virginia.

Gist became the shop boy to Lyde's agent, John Smith, in Hanover Town, so his two masters must have kept in frequent contact. Part of young Gist's role seems to have been similar to that of the son of a merchant house, going abroad to learn the practices of trading partners in order to improve business practices and help bonding between partners. John Smith's wife seems to have been born a Massie; and he was John Massie's nephew. Some of the rents to support Queen Elizabeth's Hospital were provided by an Isabella Massie for property adjoining the school's orchard, but she died in 1732, and the following year, Sarah and Ann Massie were buried. They were probably descendants of Rev. John Massey who had been school master from 1662 to his death in 1685.[38] Their surname was common in Gloucestershire to the north of Bristol; Sir William Massey had been the Parliamentarian governor of Gloucester during the Civil War before switching sides to support the king. A John Masse was uncle to Gist's master John Smith in Virginia, which may also be significant.

§

Piracy took off during the English Civil War, largely the result of

Royalists being abandoned in Jamaica, and they were forced to support themselves, they took to raiding ships. This explains the popular uniform of long coats and big wigs, typical of aristocrats at the time. It ended at the dawn of the eighteenth century, in 1701, with the execution of Captain Kidd who had been commissioned to hunt pirates but instead joined them. But their freewheeling spirit lingered in the careers of many merchants, especially those who had their own ships, and who invested in a wide range of schemes with varying levels of success. Gist's master Lyonel Lyde sen. had lived in King William County, Virginia where he married and had a son Cornelius, who became a planter, like his uncle Stephen in the same county. Several members of this family had shares in the county's iron mines and works.[39] It seems the mayor Lyde sent his son, also Lionel Lyde (1724–91) to Virginia. With his step-brother Cornelius, he traded slaves and tobacco from Copthill Court, Throgmorton Street in London. In 1765 he became a director of the Bank of England and in 1772 became a baronet, though the title died with him.[40] He owned the manor of Ayot in the county of Hertford, a convenient area for London merchants to own country retreats. He built the church there in 1787 which cost him six thousand pounds.[41] But there may have been an earlier connection, albeit a tenuous one. In 1695 John Rogers, possibly a relative of Gist's mother, and Edward Lyde were sentenced to transportation at the Taunton assizes, which covered the region south of Bristol, so included Lyde's hometown of Stanton Wick in Somerset.[42]

Being sent abroad —especially to the West Indies — was not always a death sentence. Azariah Pinney was sent to the island of Nevis for his role in the Monmouth Rebellion of 1685 which ended at the Battle of Sedgemoor after the rebels had captured Taunton. About a thousand rebels were killed and a similar number captured. The Pinney family became wealthy planters on the island. They owned a house on Great George Street in Bristol, now the Georgian House Museum. In 1831 when the Bristol riots broke out, the man who failed to quell them was a descendant, Mayor Charles Pinney.

Since the son of the mayor could not have been sent abroad as an indentured servant, it seems unlikely that this was the system under which Gist was sent to Virginia. The key term is that of merchant. Some years ago, when Bristol city centre was being redeveloped, there was a huge public outcry at the proposal that the shopping precinct its name should be the *Merchants' Quarter* as the term *merchant* allegedly celebrated slave traders. But the term referred to the profession of trading abroad, so was mostly wholesale goods, though some also kept local shops. Such international trade was the merchants' main source of income, and they often owned or invested in ships. Captains also often owned their ships in whole or part, and sometimes invested in goods, so there was considerable variation and overlap between the professions, to support each other, and to spread the risks as huge amounts of money involved. Thus, though the merchant Lyonel Lyde's son was apprenticed to a captain, it is unclear what this involved.

Some merchants travelled abroad, and could stay away for some time. But when they returned home, and their businesses expanded, they became too busy to take time out from their trade and families, so sent sons or apprentices in their stead. Ships' captains could arrange deals for them, and in some countries there were communities of English traders who acted as agents. Local philanthropist Edward Colston was the son of the merchant William; he seems to have spent some time with his family in Spain. His brother Richard became Consul in Marseilles and another was William was a resident in Lisbon where he was murdered by a fellow English merchant.[43] Many people who bought plantations in the New World stayed there long enough for them to become established before returning home, leaving agents to run them. The worst abuses of the slave system were often under absentee landlords/owners.

Bristol's population at the start of the eighteenth century was about two hundred thousand, of whom only about two hundred and fifty were granted their freedom on the basis of being merchants, though careers could change, so their numbers were far from static. Their trade guild the *Society of Merchant Venturers*, was an important and powerful group who lobbied for their interests, which they often claimed were the interests of their city and the country as a whole. They asked the government to provide protection for their ships from enemy privateers and pirates, and ransomed mariners from slavery from countries along the coast of North Africa. The society is widely reviled for campaigning for the slave trade, and is still considered to be a powerful secretive group within the city, an all male club, akin to the Freemasons, around which endless conspiracy theories circulate.

Slave trading with West Africa created a market for manufactured goods to exchange for humans, who were traded in the colonies for slave-produced crops, especially sugar, cotton and tobacco. The Africa Company was one of many established under Elizabeth to trade in set regions, so was contemporary with the Turkey Company etc. The Barbary Company traded with North Africa and imported sugar before the crop was established in the West Indies. But at the Restoration, Charles II inherited a bankrupt post-war country and his time abroad had given him a taste for Catholic-style luxury, so he helped fund his court by selling trade monopolies. The Royal Africa Company (R.A.C.) was sold a monopoly to trade with Africa, which was initially for gold, ivory and palm oil, but expanded to include slaves. But in 1698 it lost this monopoly which opened the door for other ports — especially Bristol — to move into the trade. When the R.A.C. attempted to revive their monopoly, the Society of Merchant Venturers opposed it in Parliament.[44] The South Sea Company took over the trade and attempted to establish its own monopoly in 1720, and the R.A.C. again tried to oppose provincial ports from having trading rights with Africa, threatening Bristol's merchants.. The costs of these battles in Parliament were paid by Bristol Corporation, showing the influence and importance of the Merchant Venturers. on the city. Many important men were members of both. Eventually the R.A.C. abandoned the fight and focused instead on ivory and gold trading.[45]

Given the eminence of the Lydes as merchants, they should

have been prominent in the Society of Merchant Venturers. But it seems the mayor was never a member, though two of his sons were admitted on the basis of their kinship with him. Cornelius joined in 1734 without holding office. But he was an executor to a will and guarantor for a donation of one thousand pounds to the society to build an extra wing to their almshouse on King Street. It was to accommodate six poor sailors or widows and to provide living expenses and clothing for them.[46] The addition was beside the society's Hall, but both were lost to World War II bombing. Lyonel jun. was admitted in 1746 but like his brother, held no office, and apparently had little involvement. Samuel Gist never joined, but perhaps he and the Lydes were mostly in London so the group provided little benefit to them. There are also some parallels in the lives of the elder Lyonel Lyde and Gist. While in Virginia, Lyde married and had a son, Cornelius. On the death of his wife he returned to England and remarried, with several more sons including Lyonel jun.

When he was about twenty, Samuel's master, the sixty-year-old John Smith died. This risked plunging the family into bankruptcy and destitution. Daniel Defoe claimed that the best skill a woman could learn was how to run her husband's business. Sarah may have been adept at this, but women had few legal rights, so running the family business would have been difficult or impossible on her own. Though Samuel seems to have been younger than the legal adult age, he must have learned how to run the business by then. Two years later he married Mary Smith to ensure the continuity of the family business, and to prevent neighbours gossiping about the young man living beneath the same roof as the widow, who was about ten years his senior.

The marriage of a widow to her journeyman or apprentice was common practice to ensure the continuation of businesses, and explains why so many married couples were of significantly different ages. John Smith had probably been married before, and lost a wife in childbirth, and Mary may also have had a previous marriage. Thus at the age when many of his peers were still single and completing their apprenticeships, Samuel became a businessman, a husband and step-father to Joseph and John Smith jun. He also became an executor to his late master's will, responsible for the several inheritances of the family including his wife's dowry on their marriage. The young man was forced to hit the ground running at the start of his career.

Samuel and Mary had two daughters of their own: Mary and Elizabeth. He became a burgess (freeman) of the city of Bristol in November 1752, aged approximately twenty-nine which suggests he was preparing to trade independently in the city from that date. His duties as guardian to his stepsons had expired so he advertised his intention to leave Virginia. This in turn suggests he may never have intended to settle, and that his marriage was made out of necessity rather than any mutual attraction. It seems Gist only intended to stay long enough to complete his indenture, which again marks him as different to the earlier servants who had gone to the colonies hoping to start new lives. Gist established extensive contacts with planters in Virginia, which he continued long after he returned to England.

For all its wealth, the Tidewater region where Gist was sent was largely agricultural; it must have been dull for a boy used to the bustle of a major port. His daughters, though born there, were likewise keen to move to England as soon as they were able. Yet it was Virginia that made him, that allowed him to escape what seems to have been an impoverished childhood, or at least one in which mediocrity would have been his highest expectation. Instead, he grew up to become wealthy beyond his dreams.

Gist's rise from apparent poverty seems spectacular, but it coincided with the general expansion in trade between Britain and its colonies. Land around Hanover Town where he lived was still being cleared for agriculture, with one property including a complex dam to divert water onto meadows to maximise the hay crop, so Smith's shop must have also expanded. This was an ideal environment for a young boy to learn his trade.

From about 1800 travellers in the North American colonies noted how different the children were from those of Europe. Once the colonists had cleared land and established farms, their children were allowed considerable freedom, so were unlikely to spend much time indoors with their books except when the weather forced them to. With such abundant nature on their doorsteps, they had very different childhoods to that of Gist.

It is also possible that Gist never liked his adopted homeland, though he did business with some of its most prominent men, including George Washington. He was one of the twelve eminent men who founded the Great Dismal Swamp Company to drain the land for agriculture. He was also the only one to make money from the venture as he provided the tools and slaves. But this again raised accusations against him of fraud, but not by his former colleagues.

But he was never really accepted as part of the local community, as his involvement in the Parson's Cause showed. This was a dispute over the payment of a parson's wages, which established the reputation of Patrick Henry as a great orator. Gist was the main witness in which the cleric objected to being paid in tobacco instead of money, so he demanded an increase in payments to the church, an unpopular matter. Gist played his part in local activities, serving on various committees, but his move to London suggests he never settled in the rural backwater; he probably missed the bustle of his home town. It is possible his desire to return to England made him work extra hard, to become better than good at business in order to escape.

In later years, when former neighbours from Virginia visited him in London expecting financial help from him, they were angered by his refusals. A young Virginian, Severn Eyre, arrived in London hoping to study medicine, but he was short of money and told Gist that without help he would have to return home, in response, he was informed of the next sailing. Eyre called him "an old Jew, a Turk, an Infidel".[47] In other words, an alien, whose behaviour was utterly incomprehensible. Such meanness seemed inexcusable, as Gist could easily have spared the cash. Questions were asked as to what he needed his money for, as he had no male heirs.

But Gist had worked hard from an early age, so he probably had little or no sympathy for young gentlemen who had led pampered lives. It was probably not the money, but the principle of honest hard work that made him ignore young Eyre's plea for help. It also suggests why Gist showed so much sympathy for his slaves who were forced to work so hard to support such indolent people.

4

HANOVER TOWN

When young Samuel Gist arrived in his new home in Hanover Town in Virginia it must have felt like arriving on another planet: a small, rural settlement instead of the noisy, bustling port of Bristol. American settlements — unlike those of Europe — had not evolved over time, so they served different functions for their communities. English towns were mostly centred round the parish church, which before the Reformation had been the centre of local government, and was the major landlord so was literally the heart of the community. Nearby there was often a market place with a water pump, and tools of punishment for offenders such as stocks, pillory and whipping post. For travellers there could be an inn, and for locals, a pub. Large manorial estates provided another, parallel world. They employed many people in the house and its fields, and the lord of the manor provided charity and justice as well as entertaining royalty and funding and commanding the local militia.

In Virginia, settlement began with large estates, along the river for easy transport; they continued to be the social focus for planta-tion owners and smallholders. They modelled their lives on those of the English gentry, building their own brick or stone mansions. In the Tidewater region, many had their own quays where ships could moor to load their annual tobacco crop directly, and to unload any goods that they had ordered from abroad. These estates tended to be the centres for entertaining friends and family, so residents had few reasons to visit urban centres. But they still needed to distribute produce, so Richmond had a fair, but it was a far cry from those in Europe which were often huge events for commerce, and for the various classes to interact and friends and families to keep in touch.

Col. John Page of Rosewall obtained the land of what was at the time New Kent County. By 1730 this included a tobacco warehouse called "Crutchfields" which probably included living quarters and land; within four years, its rent was fifty pounds, the highest in the county.[1] Nearby an open space seems to have become a village green, possibly used for a market.

An article from the Virginia Gazette from October 1737 describes the celebration of St Andrew's Day which was planned for the following month. It included a horse race, and competitions and prizes for cudgelling, wrestling, foot races, music and singing, for the handsomest young country maid, and the flying of a saltire flag fifty foot high.[2] This showed the newly arrived community of Scots were making a major contribution to local life. The event was funded by a benevolent bachelor to promote friendship and good society, in the hope that his fellow Scots would contribute to costs for it to continue. These were probably the same Glasgow merchants who were complained of for undercutting the English with their imports to Bristol in 1722.[3] "Scotchtown" was Patrick Henry's home when he was Governor of Virginia.[4] The presence of the Scots here shows how quickly they followed the English into the colonies after the Act of Union of 1707.

Scotland had long been an impoverished country, with poor quality, waterlogged land that was impassable in winter. They had no money to invest in colonial adventures, so had been left behind by Europe's initial expansion into the New World. Yet with a fraction of the population of its southern neighbour, they had six universities while England had only two, and from the eighteenth century the country punched well above their weight in producing some of Britain's finest and most productive law makers, educators and scientists. Many shipboard surgeons were Scots. Those who settled in North America were, like many people from impoverished countries today, largely driven by the desire to send money home to their struggling families.

In July 1695 a group of mariners including William Dampier and Basil Ringrose crossed the Isthmus of Panama. They all published accounts of their journey. Their Scottish surgeon, Lionel Wafer was injured, so stayed with a group of Indians, several of whom he successfully treated. In gratitude, they gave him some land where a species of logwood grew. Though seldom mentioned today, it was the most expensive New World product of its age. It produces a dye that varies widely in colour, depending upon the acidity or alkalinity of the water in which it is extracted. It was used by magicians and dyers, and its high tannin content also made it suitable for tanning leather. It also destroys the scent of animals, so is used by hunters to clean their traps. Dampier spent some time in the area working alongside slaves chopping down the trees and floating them on flooded rivers to the coast for export. Mills to grind it were scattered across England, including one opposite Bristol's Hotwells Spa. The mills were often named as being red, the colour of its heartwood, so often mistakenly interpreted as denoting reed beds.

Despite being warned by Wafer of the dangers of disease, the Scottish parliament decided to found a colony in the east of modern Panama, but not for the logwood trade. It was intended to become a "door of the seas, and the key to the universe". Claims were made that its eastern harbour could shelter a thousand ships, reflecting the huge levels of exotic imports flowing from Asia and South America to Europe at the time. The Scots ignored the opposition this would attract from the Spanish who were so fiercely protective of their trade that even the marooned Alexander Selkirk feared them on Juan Fernandez Island. After Selkirk was rescued, Woodes Rogers reported the castaway had long hidden from Spanish ships as he feared they would murder him or work him to death like the natives in the huge silver mines of Potosi, as he believed they were so protective of their route to the South Sea.[5]

About 20% of the wealth of lowland Scotland was invested in this venture, but their trade was blocked by the English, and the Spanish attacked them. A second attempt at settlement was abandoned in 1700 after more than two thousand men, women and children died of disease.[6] The harbour was dangerous, so again, planning had been disastrous. This reduced Scotland's fortunes even further, forcing the country to accept a financial bailout, and it joined England to join the Union with Britain in 1707. They wisely decided to invest this windfall in forming a bank. This was the Royal Bank of Scotland which in recent times went spectacularly bankrupt in the economic crash and was again bailed out by the British government. But the ports of Scotland became important centres for trade with North America, even Aberdeen on the east coast became a major centre for the spiriting away of children to fuel the Virginia tobacco trade.[7] Peter Williamson wrote an extraordinary account of his life as a victim of kidnapping and slavery which was published in 1743.[8]

Gist's new master, John Smith, was an agent for the Lyde family's multi-stranded business, so he was responsible for shipping large amounts of tobacco from surrounding estates and for importing what they could not produce, which covered everything from ribbons and beer to bricks and tombstones, which supported many local businesses in Bristol and its extensive hinterland. Thus Smith's store was a major link between the plantations and Britain, so provided an excellent education for a young man in the world of international commerce. It must have increased in him a high level of independence which served him well for the rest of his life. But as the store held a large amount of goods, it was also at risk of being broken into, or of fires breaking out. So the building included accommodation for the owner and his family, as was traditional in Britain's towns. This makes it unclear where Smith lived, as his address was generally given as being Gold's or Gould's Hill, a small two storey house on a plantation which survives several miles away.

When Smith's sons came of age, his estate was divided between them, with John jun. inheriting the shop and Joseph the plantation, though in 1773 William Anderson announced the sale of two plantations in Hanover and Goochland Counties, which could have been them.[9] They both became the property of Gist.

An advertisement in the Virginia Gazette from 1768[10] described a property in nearby King and Queen County for sale. It consisted of five hundred acres of which up to fifty was marsh, to produce hay. Its two storey brick house had four rooms per floor and large cellars for storage, with various outhouses in good condition. The land was well wooded with an orchard and large garden and was praised for its suitability for grain or tobacco. A ship of two hundred and fifty tons, a reasonably sized ocean going vessel, could moor nearby.

The ad suggested the owner could profit from the West India trade. The islands maximised their profits from exotic produce — especially sugar — by being monocultures, making self sufficiency in food impossible. This is reflected in modern Caribbean cooking which still includes items such as salt fish, rather than the plentiful fresh varieties. Grain was exchanged there for molasses which the Virginians converted into rum that they consumed, sold to ships or exported to Europe. This meant that estates in Virginia were not just trading with Britain, they were also involved in feeding other colonies, and when famines struck England in the 1760s, they exported slave-produced wheat and rice. From the mid-eighteenth century, British newspapers recommended rice to feed England's poor, as poor 'hindoos' thrived on it. Here we have the early global food chain with expensive English wheat being exported to Europe for profit, denying the poor access to it.

&.

Bristol served virtually all the slave colonies, supplying a mixture of locally manufactured goods, so a wide range of trades people in the city profited from it to some degree without actually investing in the shipping. From 1739–46, Bristol ships comprised 60% of slave voyages, fitting out thirty six ships each year, to total five hundred and fifty over this period. At the same time, Liverpool sent three hundred and eighty-nine and London three hundred and thirty-five. Isaac Hobhouse, the Bristol ship builder, and one of the city's most successful slave traders, sent slaves to Virginia, but he mostly sailed to Jamaica, from where slaves were often sent to Spanish colonies under the Asiento agreement.[11] Despite claims that both Gist and Lyde were slave traders, neither feature in lists of slave traders in Bristol, so perhaps they owned part shares, or the cargoes were mixed though it is more likely that their ships sailed from the capital.

Liverpool was more closely defined by the slave trade, as its cotton cloth was an integral link in the business chain which imported tobacco and sugar. Manufacturers in its hinterland of Lancashire imported slave-produced cotton to produce cheap cloth which was exported to clothe slaves. The cotton factories were often described as creating slave-like environments, with whole families working long hours with few breaks and little daylight. Cotton cloth also undermined domestic industries, and the cloth itself was less warm and waterproof than homespun wool, so the amount of colds and ill health in Britain's poor also increased.

But the wide range of cotton fabrics, as well as linen and silk, were popular with the elite. A pamphlet from 1782 bemoaned:

"the ladies... wear scarcely anything now but cotton, calicoes, muslin, or silks, and think no more of woollen stuffs than we think of an old almanac. We have scarcely any woollens now about our beds but blankets, and they would most likely be thrown aside, could we but keep our bodies warm without them".[12]

Thus trade for Britain was far more complex than just shuttling between two destinations — or in the case of Bristol and the West Indies — the infamous triangular trade of English manufactured goods, African slaves and slave produced goods. English merchants often chose to trade where their goods were in demand. Africans who sold slaves sometimes changed what they would accept as

payment, and colonists followed the fashions of the English aristocracy, so merchants and manufacturers had to constantly adapt to
changing demands. This was in addition to the huge risks of fitting
out ships which had to survive storms, pirates, wartime confiscations
and embargoes.

§๑

The County of Hanover was formed from Kent County in 1720
and followed the same boundaries as the parish of St Paul's. Its
main towns were Hanover and later New Castle. At Hanover Court
House, the region's most famous son Patrick Henry, orator of the
Revolution, began his career with "an impassioned plea against the
king", the Parson's Cause case of 1736[13] in which Gist was the main
witness. This was a dispute over the payment of the cleric's wages,
which for some time had been paid in tobacco, which was by then a
common form of currency in the region, in part due to the problems with fraud in notes and coins. But tobacco varied widely in
value. By the mid-eighteenth century, coin balances were popular to
test the weight of gold coins. Gist was the only witness to support
the parson, which seems to mark him as an outsider.

In 1762, shortly before Gist left for England, two tobacco warehouses faced the dock at Hanover Town, at least one of which had
foundations made of brick, probably imported from Bristol as
ballast for ships transporting tobacco. This was a huge industry, and
after the War of Independence, several brickyards in Bristol closed.
These buildings were solid, fireproof structures to store the expensive, flammable crops. It was advertised for rent in 1774 described as
"a large commodious brick store with two convenient rooms, a large
granary, a kitchen, a stable" and a fenced garden.[14]

This seems to have become the home for John Smith jun. when
he came of age, but he was struggling with the family business as
Gist wrote to him in 1768 of how "the lots where you live has cost
me a great deal of money".[15] Gist urged him to improve the houses
and land. He also advised planting fruit trees, which would make
the house more pleasant in summer, and even offered to send him

some seedlings, as he claimed that those begun the previous year had not been planted out. He even suggested that the apricots could be used to produce brandy, offering to send a still to encourage Smith, confident they would produce a profit. Gist seemed to be frustrated by his stepson's lack of success but continued to provide advice in the hope of improving the young man's situation.

He further claimed that "honor and honesty are not the only Necessary essentials for a Man of Business". He explained many other practices including investigating frequent attention into clients' accounts to ensure their businesses were viable, to prevent their shortfalls or debts damaging a man's own business. He then provided detailed business advice which should not have been necessary for a fellow trader.[16] He also complained of a six month gap in letters from Virginia, pointedly claiming that if not for information from other contacts, he would be as ignorant of affairs in Virginia as of Lapland. He claimed he was not informed as to Smith's sales, of the amount of tobacco that would be sent, and of any goods required in return, which was a similar silence to that of the previous year, which is damning. Worse, demands were being made of Lyde for payment of bills which exceeded the value of tobacco sales, so Smith was running up debts and embarrassing Gist.

Samuel pleaded with Smith to resolve the debts which could harm his reputation and his business and of Gist himself. Smith's ineptitude had become so marked that Gist believed that he would not be able to help his stepson unless the problems were promptly resolved.[17] This is all serious stuff, suggesting Smith was neglecting the most basic elements of his trade. Gist's education seems to have concentrated on writing and accurate record-keeping, but such skills seem to have been lacking in his stepson.

In 1768 Gist provided John Smith jun. with advice on crops, saying that his land was too light for a certain variety of tobacco so he should consent for it to be planted with any other suitable variety. He also recommended fertilising the fields with dung to improve yields for two to three years, so he was unwilling to sell the land for the time being.[18] This adds yet another skill the planters had to learn: land management and soil fertility, which in the region was already declining, threatening the tobacco industry. Claims were made that Gist exploited his stepsons, but he insisted they were bad at business. Yet Smith's obituary in January 1773 described him as a "Representative of Hanover", "a Merchant of Note", and "a gentleman universally loved and respected".[19]

This may have been a standard announcement, written by someone who had never met him, or it may indicate the difference in standards between Gist and his former neighbours in Hanover County. When William Anderson, as his Executor, advertised his lands for sale they included Picknocky in Hanover County of about two hundred acres complete with a dam, and two properties of five hundred and two hundred acres in Goochland.[20] Three years later a former plantation of Smiths, in King William County was also advertised for rent.[21]

But Anderson also advertised for sale the dwelling house and several lots of domestic furniture and a "likely negro manservant",[22] all of which had been made over in trust to John Smith jun. Perhaps his debts had been the result of other people's debts to him being impossible to resolve as so much money was invested in a single crop and the land to grow it. The sons may have been living in difficult times, which would probably have badly damaged even Gist's business.

One of Gist's letters to his stepson suggested he spread dung on his fields which suggests that by the 1770s the fertility of the soil was already in decline. The town thrived in the eighteenth century; but by 1845 it had almost vanished. Much of the land is now covered with corn, reflecting the above change of use. It has become the subject of archaeological investigations. The first record of the town was a warehouse built on the property of Col. John Page. It became a centre for tobacco shipments to England for the Yorktown region, so by 1734 he was paying fifty pounds per year tax on it, the highest in the county. By 1762

Page had applied for, and been granted permission, to establish a town due to the increase in commerce, but by 1766 one hundred and forty-six lots remained unsold, with the bulk of the land still in his hands, so he applied for a lottery to dispose of the remainder.

This was a common practice in England for disposing of expensive items such as ornate machinery that failed to sell via the usual methods.

Hanover Town failed to expand beyond the size of a small village and had peaked just before the outbreak of war, i.e. after Gist left. In 1774 a property was advertised which included a dwelling house, smoke house, dairy, two very good shops and even a billiard house,[23] so at least some locals were successful. Or perhaps they had bought it in expectation of becoming so. When Cornwallis passed through his troops burned the warehouses and homes of suspected rebels. In 1781 some captured British soldiers were left unguarded and embarked on apparently random acts of arson about the town. The decline of the area may have been due to developments in shipping, with larger vessels unable to make their way so far upriver. But the Pamunkey River also silted up so that by the time of the Civil War the town had become little more than a ferry crossing.

Tobacco — like sugar — cultivation drained the nutrients from the soil, so the best of the plantations were always the newest; the rest needed constant fertilising, as Gist noted in the previously mentioned letter to his stepson. This in turn reflects the benefits of plantations having a mix of crops. A letter to Gist from Roger Atkinson in 1770 claimed Peterboro was by then the best tobacco growing area, predicting that within a decade it would be producing 20,000 hogsheads, which was a third of the output of the whole county.[24]

This seems to confirm that production from the James River area was in decline. Large numbers of animals, especially hogs, provided manure to maintain soil fertility, as did annual flooding which brought nutrient rich mud onto the fields. The rise in importance and wealth of the West Indies' trade and Britain's growing population encouraged the planting of corn, which was first imported to Bristol in response to the famine of 1725/6. By the 1770s properties advertised for sale were often a mix of woodland, grazing and arable lands, praised for being largely self-sufficient. This further suggests that when Gist's slaves were waiting to be resettled, they could have supported themselves, relieving executors of much need to supervise them and preventing them being a financial liability to the community.

Gist left no diaries though he is mentioned in accounts by others. His family has become extinct, so little survives to provide a framework to reconstruct his life in Virginia, nowhere for scholars or tourists to visit and engage with the period. William Anderson lived at Dundee in Virginia from 1778. The plantation was settled by John Smith sen., who built the house about 1768 but only the brick foundations remain.[25] Gold's — or Gould's — Hill survives: a surprisingly small two-storey building, made of bricks, probably imported from Bristol. It is a far cry from the log cabins where the slaves were housed, but also distant from the grand mansions of slave plantations that now feature on historical and tourist trails in the Deep South.

5

THE INSURANCE BUSINESS

Gist returned to Britain in 1768 but it is unclear what kind of business he was involved in. He had become a burgess, or freeman, of Bristol in 1752, and when he purchased Wormington Grange in 1787 he was described as a Bristol merchant.[1] He was part or full owner of several ships, and traded in slaves but apparently with little success. In 1774 the Bristol Poll Book listed him as a merchant in Aldgate, London. This address was America Square, which was — like the shop where he trained in Virginia — both business and residential. He began a second career, an extension of the others, by dealing in stocks and insurance.

In Britain, under the Normans, markets were held within walking distance of everyone, so usually about seven miles apart. They were often held at crossroads, and stone crosses were built to mark the spot and provide steps to display the wares. Some city churches such as Temple and All Saints in Bristol, had tolzeys, or meeting places for payment of market tolls, with colonnades along their walls for rent and to provide shelter for traders. As commerce expanded, Thomas Gresham built London's Royal Exchange in 1570 as a place for businesspeople and merchants to congregate and make deals. When architectural historian Nikolas Pevsner was discussing England's toleration of her various religious groups, he cited Voltaire who claimed:

> "All denominations meet on the Exchange — the only ones called infidels are those who go bankrupt."[2]

But when proposals were made for an enclosed market in the early eighteenth century in Bristol, traders opposed the scheme as it went against their notions of open, fair trading. Or perhaps they were too poor or mean to pay the extra tolls. The architect John Wood of Bath mocked them for their ignorance and their preference for having themselves and their goods exposed to and damaged by the weather. When servants arrived in Virginia, they were reported to be sold on board the ships to recompense the costs of their passage. Slave markets were held at quaysides when ships arrived in ports

The insurance industry began in the Italian city states, so merchants could spread the risks of individual voyages. It was introduced to England by Mediterranean traders and was often a sideline for merchants, as a form of mutual support and to spread risks. Coffee houses were established in London from the mid-seventeenth century and soon became popular places for specialist groups of men to meet, socialise, read aloud newspapers and discuss their shared interests. Their popularity was fuelled by the housing shortage in the aftermath of the Great Fire, when few people had sufficient space to entertain at home. Coffee houses were cheaper and quieter than taverns; a man could spend a whole day there for the price of a cup of coffee.

By Gist's time, they had taken on a life of their own. They

brought together men of different ranks and professions, gave opportunities for the circulation of information and allowed investors to meet venturers and to feel safe handing over money to them Notices of auctions, sales and entertainments were posted on the walls; news and rumours were circulated. In 1675 Charles II closed them due to fears of them spreading sedition, but this caused such an outcry they were reopened only days later, on condition that no scandalous papers or topics were discussed there.

Like cheap or less formal versions of Victorian gentlemen's clubs, they became centres of urban —but of course strictly male — social life. By the time of Queen Anne there were about five hundred in London, with specialist groups patronising houses near to their places of business.[3] Doctors and clerics met at Child's, the fashionable set descended on the Royal Coffee House at Charing Cross, and businessmen met near the Royal Exchange. The "universal liberty of speech of the English nation" uttered amid clouds of tobacco smoke, with equal vehemence whether against the government and the Church, or against their enemies, had long been the wonder of foreigners; it was the quintessence of coffee-house life.[4]

They also became popular meeting places for various merchant groups trading with the various colonies: Chesapeake from 1677, New York from the 1690s etc. Pennsylvania was mostly settled by Quakers, who kept in touch via their meeting houses. Coffee houses were used for mail collection, and though not initially political, when necessary, they could become foci for gathering support for petitions to the Privy Council or Board of Trade.[5] Most were father and son businesses, like the Lydes, which explains whey they and Gist left so few traces. The members of the Virginia mercantile lobby were mostly close relatives of planters, reflecting the many intertwining family links found throughout the colonial records. In 1728 the French forced down tobacco prices so a meeting by London merchants agreed a minimum price at the Black Swan Tavern, behind the Royal Exchange.[6]

Ned Ward's Weekly Shopkeeper of 1706 described how he spent his busy day:

"rise at 5; counting-house till 8; then breakfast on toast and Cheshire cheese; in his shop for two hours, then a neighbouring coffee house for news; shop again, till dinner at home (over the shop) at 12 on a 'thundering joint' ; 1 o'clock on Change; 3, Lloyd's Coffee House for business; shop again for an hour; then another coffee house (not Lloyd's) for recreation, followed by 'sack shop' to drink with acquaintances, till home for a 'light supper' and so to bed, before Bow Bell rings nine."[7]

Though this was decades before Gist's arrival, it shows how complex the business of business was, and how much social activity was required.

Not far to the south of the Exchange were the international docks where ships arrived. The famous Lloyd's insurance brokers began in a coffee house near Tower Street which became a first port of call when overseas ships' captains arrived to settle their business with investors, merchants and insurers, and to pass on their news. Early newspapers carried no commercial or shipping news, so information spread by word of mouth. Lloyd's had a pulpit for holding auctions of ships and cargoes, including those of the Admiralty, and for reading out the latest shipping information. The proprietors established a network of contacts in ports around Britain, which they published as the first Lloyd's Lists. Customers could read and discuss news and newspapers, and ads were displayed on the walls, some of which were for indentured servants to the colonies, so they played at least a marginal role in the spiriting away of the poor from Britain.

The Great Fire of London in 1666 triggered a boom in fire insurance and the construction of fireproof buildings. By the end of the seventeenth century, trade to the Americas had expanded, so ships became larger and more expensive and their goods also rose in value. Marine insurance became an important means of spreading and sharing the risks, but what seemed to be easy profits in turn encouraged the entry of less experienced investors who were more inclined to become involved in high risk investments. Thus, habitués of the coffee shops became better informed on marine matters than the government, which in turn led to the authorities sharing information with them on international and naval affairs, helping them reduce their own risks and maximise profits. Many politicians were also merchants, who passed laws to protect their own interests, but since commerce was seen as being of benefit to the nation, this was never treated as a problem.

Such close links between business and government are widely condemned today, and can be illegal. But at the time, the government and royalty struggled for funding, so encouraging trade increased taxation, which paid for the navy that protected shipping, and was claimed to be of benefit to the wider community.

Marine insurance expanded to become a major industry following the Smyrna disaster of 1693 when the French attacked a convoy of Dutch and English merchants escorted by their navies. Ninety ships were lost, and forty captured. It was the worst catastrophe for the City of London since the Great Fire and bankrupted some of the City's top merchants.[8] Many early marine insurers were former employees of the East India Company, who were able to put their extensive knowledge of foreign shipping to productive use.[9] Lloyds Coffee House held auctions of ships and cargoes, including those of the Admiralty, so brought together a wide range of men from the world of government and commerce, though the two realms often overlapped.

The rise in insurance followed the carnage of the English Civil War, when many educated people had been killed or fled, making space for the rise of a generation of newly rich but inexperienced investors who were easy targets for promoters of the most outrageous schemes. In 1720 over a hundred schemes were declared illegal, and many more should have been.[10] The Restoration reintroduced many European habits, such a high spending on luxury goods and there was a huge rise in the culture of gambling, with people betting on anything from horse racing to the date of death of a famous person. Scores of mining schemes found support, most of which were frauds. Britain's wars with France and Spain in the latter part of the eighteenth century were largely over commerce; with no clear plan or strong leadership, she blundered into war against her North American colonies, but by the early nineteenth century, when Gist died, Britain had become the world's largest economy, with her own colonies that she had settled, others torn from the hands of the French, and those abandoned by Spain.

Investment in high risk ventures helped create a boom and bust economy. In the early eighteenth century the population suffered a form of frenzy, in which many gambled and invested in the most far fetched ventures, never thinking that they could fail. Pepys sometimes invested, Defoe was ruined by it. But it was also a time of debunking of myths, and major achievements in exploration. Debates about the existence of a southern land to balance the mass of Europe were settled with the return of William Dampier from his discovery of Australia. Tales of strange creatures from abroad had long been accepted; as late as 1766 Commander Byron returned with tales of Patagonian giants, at the same time that Captain Cook's discoveries were filling in the remaining gaps on the globe, many of which still stand today. The truth often seemed more incredible than myth, so people struggled to separate the two.

Out of this environment emerged the extraordinary South Sea Bubble, when shares attracted so much investment the company took over the national debt. The public trusted the managers to know what they were doing, but the huge sums allowed the stock to take on a life of its own before its spectacular collapse. For careful investors it provided a timely warning, and showed the wisdom of not putting all one's eggs in a single basket. Many of the losers were ruined; some went to sea to escape the shame, and to attempt to restore their finances by pursuing other pipe dreams

Marine insurance boomed throughout the eighteenth century, even during wartime, as — bizarrely — Britons were allowed to insure enemy ships, so whichever side won, the insurers generally made profits. When Admiral Rodney captured the tiny island of St Eustatius, a major entrepôt for West Indian trade, in 1781, British underwriters screamed in pain when forced to pay the huge insurance claims of the enemy.[11] Such practices led to accusations that the insurers were disloyal, but their profits helped pay for the British government, and thus the navy.

Another anomaly was the lack of standard forms for policies, so many would not have stood up in court. But the practice of genteel behaviour and gentlemanly honour reduced the risk of disputes, though there were occasional examples of fraud. From 1779, policies were produced using a standard printed format, which is still — with obvious alterations to account for changing conditions — the standard for today's policies. Its strength lies in its clarity so that all those involved know and agree to what they are signing.[12]

After the Reformation, European trade became divided, with the Protestant nations of northern Europe and England being forced to seek new markets. Under Elizabeth, English merchants settled in Istanbul and they sent exotic items such as silk and tapestries home, reducing the demand for wool which had long been the mainstay of England, especially the West Country. This was due to the huge flocks of sheep that had been introduced to the uplands by the Normans. Once England established colonies in the New World, a series of Navigation Acts were passed which forced the colonies to send their goods only in English ships. This helped expand her maritime trade, and to train sailors as merchant ships were converted to military uses during war time. Support for the slave trade was often based on claims that its ships were the nursery for the navy. But most of the naval battles were to protect merchant shipping. The West Indies became known as the cockpit of Europe.

This monopoly on shipping was widely resented, especially by the ship owners of the northern American region where ship-building was a major industry. Imports to Britain were taxed, which helped local tradesmen, but again was resented by colonists for increasing the cost of their goods. This also increased the cost in Europe for colonial goods — especially sugar and tobacco — which in turn helped fuel trade disputes with Europe. From the middle of the century, wars were waged over trade supremacy; Pitt was determined to destroy French trade and prevent its recovery.[13] Britain would also have attacked Spain but it brought about its own destruction. Failure to invest its colonial wealth led to its empire collapsing after the Napoleonic Wars, and Britain was the only European nation wealthy enough to pick up the pieces.

Underwriting ships in wartime was the highest of all risks; fortunes could be made or lost overnight, even by the most experienced of traders. Throughout the War of Independence, the main focus was on land battles across the Atlantic, but there were less famous risks from privateers trading with the Baltic area, which provide crucial supplies for the navy such as masts and hemp for ropes. John Paul Jones became a hero to the North Americans for his plunder of British shipping in the North Sea and New England ships took over three thousand British ships between 1776 and '83, some of which were recaptured or redeemed.[14] Until 1769 Lloyds would underwrite any risk, and members made huge profits from the Seven Years' War which ended in 1763 But peace saw profits decline along with interest from inexperienced investors. Walpole described it as a form of game, "a more solemn species of [the card game] Hazard".[15]

The original Lloyds Coffee House became too small, so it moved to the Royal Exchange in 1774. Membership cost a mere two pounds per year subscription; and extra funding came from catering profits and sales of Lloyd's List.[16] But as membership was open to anyone, it attracted many inexperienced members, so the older, more established businessmen remained at the old site. It is possible that established trans-continental merchants such as Gist and the Lydes continued to trade amongst themselves and had little or no need for new arrangements.

§♣

Gist returned to England in 1765 and settled in London, at Savage Gardens near the Tower of London and close to the Customs House and the quays, so he could easily keep up to date with overseas shipping. The Exchange, where he traded tobacco, and the surrounding coffee houses where shipping contracts were made and insurance carried out were about a mile westwards.

Samuel became a successful member of the community involved in the buying and selling of shares, but especially in marine insurance. His work at Smith's shop had involved contact with ships captains and owners — often the same person — and assessing the risks of safety for the shipment of his own goods and of imports. He was a founder of the Dismal Swamp Company; he purchased a ship and imported slaves for the project, as well as providing tools and other supplies. He thus became the only shareholder of the disastrous project to make any money from it, but he seems to have been the most actively involved in it. He seems to have followed a similar career to that of the Lydes, who were based in Throgmorton Street, and who also owned several ships. Gist had purchased a ship named after his daughters, the Mary and Elizabeth which allowed him to cut out the middle men, by trading directly with Hanover Town.[17]

Shortly after Gist's return, in 1769 Thomas Fielding set up a new Lloyd's Coffee House in Pope's Head Alley, still near the Exchange. It aimed to make the industry more professional, but the building was old, so they moved to large, well lit rooms in the Royal Exchange itself, placing them at the very centre of the nation's business community. It was founded by seventy nine subscribers. One source claims Gist was among them,[18] but many records were lost when the Exchange burned down in 1838. Lifetime membership required a payment of only fifteen pounds, but Gist's name does not appear in any of their surviving records, which raises questions as to his role in insurance.

It could be that Gist arrived in the UK with his own extensive colonial connections so had no need for such an organisation. Many colonists who settled in London were concentrated in Marylebone where Gist's eldest daughter Mary lived with her second husband, Martin Pearkes, a tobacco merchant whose family had traded with the Smith store. They are buried together in the chapel of St John's Wood, Regent's Park, so it is possible Gist traded among this community rather than the wider world at Lloyds. There were many insurers who continued to trade on the Exchange itself and in smaller offices in surrounding streets, especially Pope's Head Alley. The area was also a magnet for a wide range of travelling shows demonstrating science and technology, some of which found funding amongst the traders, so their interests were diverse. The other London centre for such entertainments was at Charing Cross, a focus for the idle rich.

Gist avoided the disaster of the attack on British shipping in the convoy of East and West Indian ships in August 1780. A French and Spanish fleet took fifty-five of the sixty-three ships. The estimated loss was a staggering one and a half million pounds, which came close to bankrupting the industry and Lloyds itself.[19] Many individual traders were bankrupted but Gist was untouched, which led to suggestions he had insider information.

When Woodes Rogers and Dampier attacked the Spanish treasure ships, they had been hunting for the marine equivalent of a needle in a haystack. But such a huge fleet with its escorts was a much easier target. More likely, he was a very conservative man; those who lost were probably young, inexperienced and/or reckless.

The British were at war with their European neighbours for nearly a century till the end of the French Wars, and with North America twice between 1775 and 1815. This created a huge rise in demand for marine insurance, which corresponds with Gist's involvement in the trade, just as his time in Virginia corresponded with the rise in interest in tobacco and land there. So in part, his fortune was based on being in the right place at the right time. By the start of the nineteenth century, the average earnings of an underwriter was about forty thousand pounds per year, with profits of about 50% or higher.[20] This makes it one of the most lucrative businesses ever, but in order to make such sums, a man had to have plenty in order to cover losses, so it was not a career for the poor or faint hearted. At the end of the wars Britain's mercantile goals had been achieved as

Britain by then owned a staggering eleven twelfths of the world's shipping.

Premiums were based on risk, but situations were constantly in flux. Allegiances changed whilst ships were at sea; they might arrive in what they believed to be a safe port only to be impounded by the authorities on the basis that they were enemies. Even if mistakes of false arrest were admitted, compensation was rarely forthcoming. When privateers were successful, they often ransomed the captured ship and its cargo in order to continue the pursuit of further prey, so the claiming of prizes and insurance was also complicated. For a man like Gist who had never served in battle, this was probably the next best thing, a game of risk which promised huge rewards for the right people.

As help for most of the many injured combatants and their families was in short supply, Lloyds became a major source of charity. They forged close bonds with the merchant navy and often raised huge sums simply by announcing a collection in the main trading room.[21] Their members set up the first soup kitchen at Spitalfields at the start of the nineteenth century, which seems a far cry from its trade, but this area of East London was close to the docks, so provided much of the manpower for Britain's navy and merchant fleets, as well as dockworkers. This was long before the welfare state, and the men were only paid when in employment so the combatants suffered when peace was declared.

Peace was often feared by the authorities as it would signal a surge in crime. Members of Lloyds were thanked by Nelson for establishing a fund for distressed seamen, and he often sent them inside information in return. Lloyds also designed and established the first of what became lifeboats in 1785, one of which was rowed by Northumberland's famous heroine Grace Darling who helped rescue the crew of a trawler.[22] But the great defender of the rights of common people, William Cobbett complained of Lloyd's usurping the Crown's powers and acting without democratic oversight, so they were akin to modern outsourcing companies.

Slave traders also acquired a reputation for their generosity to good causes. Bristol's most infamous resident was the merchant and slave trader Edward Colston, who was famous not just for his wealth, but for giving most of it away, earning him a place in the *Encyclopaedia Brittanica*. Like Gist, he did so via his will, but claims were made that he had given away huge sums throughout his lifetime. When urged to marry, he allegedly claimed "every helpless widow is my wife and her distressed orphans my children.[23] Like Gist, much of his wealth was in government consols, a popular form of stocks which provided income for the government's wars, which supported the expansion of trade, and they were secure.

Colston was said to have given three thousand pounds to Ludgate debtors, Whitechapel Prison and the Marshalsea, a thousand pounds to the poor of Whitechapel and dispensed beef and broth to the poor of his own neighbourhood, so his largesse a century before Gist's death was huge. He was involved in the Royal Africa Company, so has been demonised in his home town of Bristol, with demands for his statute to be removed. He was born into a wealthy family of long standing; they owned a large house in the centre of the city and they traded with Spain and Portugal. Edward had a long successful career in trade before he retired to Mortlake where he died. Though he seems to have left Bristol as a young man and seldom returned, his founding of several schools and almshouses there, in addition to many London charities truly puts him in a league of his own. Like Gist, he had a long life, and left no direct male heirs, as he never married.

Gist was also involved in charitable work and a large part of his will involved the details of his many legacies. He attended several annual dinners for the Society of Ancient Britons, founded in 1715 as a loyalist body to distance the Welsh from any Jacobite associations. Wales had no major towns in the eighteenth century, so many Welsh people settled in England and further afield. Bristol had a successful Society of Ancient Britons which supported the poor of their community through an annual feast. In London, it built a school on Clerkenwell Green, (now the Marx Memorial Library) before it moved to Grays Inn Lane.[24] Gist attended the annual feast on St David's Day in 1809 when the gents breakfasted at the schoolhouse, then travelled to St Anne's Church, Soho, where prayers were read in Welsh, then to Carleton House to greet their patron, the Prince of Wales before ending at an inn where they were joined by nobles including their patron who donated a hundred and five pounds. The Duke of Northumberland gave a hundred pounds and Gist contributed a mere five guineas. The total raised that day was one thousand and eighteen pounds, sixteen shillings, which was applied to educate poor Welsh children.[25] In 1813 the thanksgiving service was held at St George's church, Hanover Square, one of the most fashionable of London's churches, before the rest of the day's celebrations and fundraising.

In 1797 Gist was Chairman of the Gloucester Society of London, founded to encourage gents of the county to fund apprenticeships for deserving poor children of the county. Chairmen tended to be the great and the good of the county. The physician Edward Jenner, discoverer of a treatment for smallpox based on cowpox also served, as did the wealthy planter of Barbados and founder of a college and library at Oxford, Christopher Codrington. The charity was funded by annual subscriptions of one guinea, and collections during the annual dinner. Like many charities of the time, these societies provided social and networking opportunities to encourage the benevolence of members.

In 1785, Gist became a lifetime governor for the Royal London Hospital, the only one to serve the east of London.[26] in the company of the Duke of Devonshire and John William Anderson of Charterhouse Square near Gist's home, which was probably his son in law, or one of his many brothers. Donations were apparently collected to establish a medical school at the hospital which attracted the support of large numbers of the country's great and good. The President was HRH the Duke of Gloucester, the king's son. Though several hospitals served the western area of London, this was the only one established in the East End. Joseph Merrick lived there, and Dr. Barnardo who founded the children's charity of his name trained there. It is now one of the most respected medical research institutes in the country.

6

GIST'S WILL

Few records survive of Samuel's long and remarkable life, though his occasional appearances in the lives of his more famous friends and colleagues offer tantalising hints. In 1769 he signed a petition to the king condemning the behaviour of the radical politician John Wilkes, who gained widespread support for opposing the government policy of increasing taxes on the colonies.[1] This has led to suggestions that Gist opposed American interests. But Wilkes was a radical, and popular with the infamous Georgian mob, so he threatened economic stability in a time of increasing chaos on both sides of the Atlantic. Gist served on a committee of Virginia merchants who petitioned the House of Commons in 1775.[2]

Though entitled to vote in national elections from 1752, Gist only made the journey to Bristol to do so twice. In 1774 he supported Henry Cruger, the Princeton-educated merchant who is unique in having served in both local and national office in Britain and North America. He supported appeasement, which suggests Gist was not hostile to the American colonies. Parliament was dissolved in autumn 1774. Whigs in Bristol disapproved of their longstanding MP Robert Nugent, Lord Clare: an Irishman who became famous for repeatedly marrying rich women who conveniently died. As a result, he amassed huge wealth and the method of his rise became known as *Nugentism*. But he supported the king's aggression towards the American colonies, so despite many years serving the city, plying voters with food and drink, and benevolently importing shiploads of grain during famines, he lost support. The great orator, and another Irishman, Edmund Burke was in search of a seat, but lacked the wealth to run his own campaign, so was approached by several wealthy Bristolians — mostly Quakers — to stand. He was also supported by the evangelist and abolitionist Hannah More. Traditionally the city voted for a local member who understood local people and a national figure to promote them in parliament; MPs were generally chosen via local agreement so the polls were a foregone conclusion, but in Bristol they were often disputed, and hence expensive. After weeks of argumentative campaigning, Cruger and Burke were elected.

Bribery was common in elections; nominees spent huge sums on entertainment, travel and accommodation for supporters to attend and to vote. The daughters of freemen were said to marry strangers to allow them to vote, with the couples separating soon after, a practice believed to be legal. Costs for MPs in Bristol ran to thousands of pounds, and the city was often held up as a reason to reject suffrage by northern towns such as Manchester which at the time had no franchise. Claims were made at this election that four hundred voters were brought from London, and even one from South Carolina. Given Gist's lack of interest in elections prior to this, he may have been energised by the threat to his business that the war with North America posed. Local merchant Matthew Brickdale disputed the close outcome, but was quashed. Burke made no friends at the outset by refusing to participate in the triumphant procession by Cruger through the city streets. Burke's worldliness and support for issued that were against local interests such as supporting Catholic emancipation ensured he was not nominated again. Cruger was later praised for his lucid speeches on American affairs.[3]

Gist voted a second time in 1781, another hotly contested election to replace an MP who had died. Cruger was by then being condemned as a "foreigner", not helped by his presence in New York when nominations opened. Arguments raged over whether he was still a British citizen. His supporters retorted that his rival Daubney supported the Jacobites in 1745. Over a thousand new voters were admitted as freemen. Both candidates hired mobs of supporters who, fuelled by free alcohol, repeatedly clashed in the streets. Daubney won, but soon after, sailors fired on a rioting crowd causing several deaths.[4] Gist voted for Matthew Brickdale, a former woollen draper and one of the richest men in Bristol, who had a long career in politics. This suggests Gist's attitude towards the colonies had shifted. In Virginia he had risked losing the lands he had worked so hard to acquire, and his battle to secure them led locals to accuse him of being a traitor. But for Gist — like other successful businessmen — the only thing that really mattered to him was the colour of a person's money. This belief also lay at the heart of the expansion of the British Empire.

In 1768 Gist's underage eldest daughter eloped to Scotland with William Anderson, the eldest son of a Virginian family of long standing. This was an act about which Gist wrote to his stepson John Smith jun.: "I have not seen her & sincerely hope I never shall as she has almost killed me by this act of undutifulness".[5] But when he risked having his American property confiscated during the war, his heart seems to have mended, as he needed William and Mary to save his estate. This made him no friends there and placed the couple in a difficult situation of divided loyalties.

Even allowing for Samuel Gist's long life and work history, his will is huge. It marches across sixteen closely written pages, with little punctuation, and ending in codicils squashed into the margins. In American sources, this translates into "58 closely written pages".[6] It is a hard read and must have been difficult to write, as the world continued to change, even between his original version of 22 June 1808 and the final version of January 1815. The final document has been described as rambling, but this was due to his attempt to allow for all contingencies, and ensure his intentions were carried out.

Yet it is still scattered with errors and omissions, some of which seem uncharacteristic in his neglect of important details. It seems he should have done his research better: it was not as if the Grim Reaper struck without warning. Though a suggestion was made that he should retire when he turned sixty, he continued in robust health. After such a busy life in commerce, his friends were probably all business associates, and with no grandchildren, there was likely no other way for him to pass his time. He continued to purchase land even after he wrote his will, so the document was still a work in progress up to his end. Despite all his efforts, there were still matters left unresolved, which caused problems for his heirs and executors in the years that followed.

His will is the only personal document left behind by Gist, so it is invaluable in providing clues to his life and some insight into what drove this extraordinary man. Though his daughters had no children, Mary adopted two orphan relatives of her husband who became her main heirs. Gist's rejection of them to continue his name shows bloodlines, however tenuous, were crucial to him. He had had plenty of time to choose a male heir but by his death he was largely ignorant of the survival of many of his relatives, so he had failed to keep in touch with them. This may have been reasonable when he lived in Virginia, but on his return to England, he could have made the necessary enquiries. There is no mention of any legacies to friends in Bristol, so he must have lost contact with any school friends on his departure, apart from the Lydes.

After Gist died, his executors advertised in the press for information on his cousin James Gist and discovered he had gone to India decades earlier. This suggests he was, like Gist, from a poor but respectable family had sought his fortune abroad. But it was eventually established that he — like so many young men in late eighteenth century Britain — saw his hopes end in an early grave in the

tropical heat and diseases of India. He left no issue. Why did
Samuel not investigate this before he wrote his will? In the electoral
lists for Bristol, there was a Thomas Gist, a weaver who lived in
Somerset Street, Whitechapel, London, not far from Samuel at
America Square, Aldgate. This is unlikely to have been a coincidence, and again, enquiries could — and should — have been made
by him. If this Thomas was a close relative, did Gist resent him for
not caring for him as a child? But if so, why leave any money to
his son?

Gist's will provides a window for us onto the life of Gist the
orphan, a term which referred to the loss of at least one parent, as a
married couple were seen as an inseparable unit, with neither being
able to survive without the other. A widow could not support her
family, and a widower could not work and care for his children. Gist
seemed to have had no family beyond his daughters, but in his will
he left legacies for a surprisingly numerous list of cousins. After
noting his Gist cousins on his father's side, he records several from
his mother's family, the Rogers. A daughter of the late John Rogers
of London was left one hundred pounds, and the late Henry
Rogers' son Samuel was given Gist's clothes plus fifty pounds, a
similar legacy to that of a loyal servant, suggesting they knew each
other, and perhaps the young man had been named after his
wealthy relative in hope of preferment. There were also legacies to
an aunt who seems to have married a Mr Onion, though Gist did
not know their Christian names, and a John Williams, apparently
the son of his mother's sister Elizabeth from the Rogers family.

But the main legatees were children of yet another Rogers aunt,
the Sellicks: John Sellick was left a hundred pounds per year, and his
brother Josiah eventually inherited the bulk of Gist's estate after it
had passed, domino-like, through his daughters Mary Pearkes and
Elizabeth Fowkes.

This suggests that Josiah was the eldest brother; following the
law of primogeniture which kept estates together rather than
sharing them among all children. This is why so many younger sons
of elite families entered the military and the Church as they were
excluded from sizeable inheritances. But this was not always the

case, especially if the children were born over a long span of time. Gist's son-in-law William Anderson was the eldest son of David Anderson of Virginia, who left most of his land to his youngest son. It seems the older brothers had already been given help and financial support to establish businesses and families. In the will of Philippa Walton of Waltham Abbey Gunpowder Works, she left most of the family wealth to her daughters on the basis that her sons had already received so much from the family business during their lives.[7] Men were able to work and support themselves and their families, whereas what little employment was available for women was for low pay, hence women tend to be prominent as legatees in wills.

Gist provided some interesting detail, by bequeathing John Sellick one hundred pounds per year, but this amount was to be reduced to fifty if he continued his "idle life" instead of pursuing an honest livelihood. Of all Gist's potential heirs, it seems that Josiah stood out as a safe pair of hands to preserve his inheritance. This in turn suggests that Gist may have been seen as a reliable child, so was chosen to be sent abroad. Or in the absence of a family business to inherit, this offered him a chance to establish his own. But there was another factor in Gist's choice. In 1774, Phripp, Taylor & Co had asked Gist to provide them with a reliable apprentice for their store,[8] which was a post similar to that which had launched Gist's own career. He sent a relative with the surname of Sellick, probably the father of Josiah and John.

Like Gist, the surname Sellick or Sellick is uncommon, though like the Lydes who came from Stanton Wick, it seems to have been a Somerset name. Josiah was an accountant on Hotwells Road in 1793 so seems to have had similar training to Gist, perhaps even in anticipation of the inheritance. The surname appears in an unflattering light during the Civil War when Ireland was devastated and the country massively depopulated by violence, disease and forced emigration. Irish lands were sequestered to pay the cost of Cromwell's war. In 1653 a licence was issued to ship five hundred "natural" Irish people to America, and many thousands of others followed. Boston merchants were involved, including a Sellick.[9]

$\mathcal{S}$

Gist's reputation for unscrupulous dealings seems to have been undermined by his mention of a disputed bill of exchange for three hundred and fifty pounds with a John Hiscock of Virginia. Gist must have had regrets over this as he left this amount to the man's heirs. He also made amends with his former manager John Tabb. He also mentioned another longstanding matter concerning "a parcel of indentured servants" consigned to William Anderson by John Wilkinson of Stockton. Gist claimed to have lost the paperwork, but thought they had not been paid for. He left a hundred pounds to pay the debt, inviting Wilkinson's heirs to contact his executors to make good any shortfall. This matter seems to have involved Wilkinson having leased two ships to the British government to transport troops in 1775.[10] Gist's ship the *Mary*, was one of them, and a letter in the press claimed that Gist must have known of this crime. If so, he failed to admit it in his will. His crime seems to have been the transportation of British troops. But this was before war broke out, and as convicts were sometimes forced to fight, it may have begun as a legitimate contract.

Again, why did Gist leave this matter unresolved? Was Anderson importing indentured servants to replace the slaves he intended to free? Or had conditions changed so fast during the war that someone changed the nature of people who were shipped? Given the amount of overlap between prisoners, servants and the armed forces, the boundaries between the rights and treatment of the various transportees could be fluid, especially in war time. And yet Wilkinson's will, written in 1797 is a tedious list of stocks to be left to his sons and other heirs. There is no mention of this affair, as it must have been long forgotten by this wealthy industrialist. Or perhaps he had better things to do with his time than to lock horns with the disputatious Gist. This matter also highlights how complex trade and social connections could be at the time, with a business venture that linked London, Stockton and Virginia.

Samuel's reputation as a miser is also challenged by his possession of a dinner service bearing his family crest; he also had a service owned by William Anderson which should have been in the possession of his widow, Gist's eldest daughter, Mary. Samuel owned silver dishes and candlesticks, suggesting he enjoyed entertaining, as was common for men in commerce at the time. The image of Gist as a loner is thus not sustainable, as London merchants spent much of their time exchanging news amongst themselves and socialising in order to understand and trust each other. This was largely developed through social occasions, especially after dinner when the ladies would retire, leaving the men to their port and cigars and talk of worldly matters.

In order to have become such a successful merchant, Gist must have had formidable social skills. A modern media mogul was once described as being able to charm you out of your underwear without you noticing. Gist only seems to have made enemies of people who could not help him, i.e. his debtors. Amongst people who mattered, he was probably a networker of the highest level.

The will recognised his eldest daughter's rights to the land she and her husband had held for him during the Revolutionary War, which had been vested in her by an act passed in the Virginia House of Burgesses in 1782. He had been paying her five hundred pounds per year on condition that she surrendered all claims to the land. He increased this legacy to fifteen hundred per year, but if she refused to surrender the lands, she was to receive only a shilling. On her death, this legacy was to go to her sister and on her demise, to their cousin Josiah Sellick.

This part of the will has often been cited as applying to both daughters, but Elizabeth had played no role in managing the properties. Mary had returned to Virginia when she married against her father's wishes. Had she been a dutiful daughter, she would have remained in London, and Gist would likely have lost all his North American lands. Gist's offer was a clever means of challenging the act passed in the House of Burgesses in Virginia which had vested the lands in Mary. Elizabeth would have been provided with a generous dowry when she married, which was held by trustees and invested safely. Mary's elopement meant she was deprived of this sum. Both daughters seem to have married well, though William Anderson seems to have been hampered as well as helped by his wealthy father in law. Each daughter had received four hundred and eighty pounds per year, paid out of Gist's British lands, and on his death they acquired an extra one thousand five hundred and twenty pounds per year. When the first daughter died, her share passed to the second, which finally eventually descended to Josiah Sellick.

Throughout his life, Gist was involved in several charities, most of which received the bulk of their income from annual dinners, again reflecting Gist's gregarious nature. It is impossible to know whether his benefactions were given due to his benevolence, or his enjoyment of an evening of alcohol-fuelled dining in the company of other affluent gents. He may have donated to other causes whose records have not been traced. In his will, he provided a list of those he favoured, which shines a light on the man's interests. Like most men in the early financial services industry, his money tended to be in the form of government consuls.

Gist's bequests were mostly to London charities, many of which were to help the poor, especially by promoting their education and training. But the biggest was ten thousand pounds to maintain six poor men and six poor women in Bristol, and for six boys to be funded to attend his alma mata, Queen Elizabeth's Hospital, and for four poor girls to become servants and four boys to be apprenticed. They were all to be of Bristol families, but not in receipt of alms, meaning they were of low income, but not in poverty; apparently like his own parents, they were the working poor. He left a hundred pounds each to various charities including Bristol Royal Infirmary, and others were in London: Christ's Hospital, the (Royal) London Hospital and the Lying-In [maternity] Hospital, the Welsh Charity School, the Hospital for the Blind, the Marine Institution, which may have been the Bristol institution which was founded in 1785 to educate poor boys to serve at sea.[11] His gift to the Hospital for Deserted Young Children may have been to the famous Foundling Hospital, established by Captain Coram and supported by Handel, Hogarth and many other famous London-ers. It was near St George's Church, several blocks from his house in Gower Street. What is strikingly absent from this list is a mention of any religious groups, although most of the charities he supported often attended church services in the company with the beneficiaries, before their annual dinners.

Gist should have attended a parish church near his home, St Giles' in the Fields, known as the parish church associated with Byron and the Shellys, but it was also the setting for Hogarth's Gin Lane. It seems to have been very high Anglican which may have been a problem for him, or the presence of a plague pit in its churchyard may have deterred him from being buried there. His insistence that his slaves be educated in the Anglican Church suggests he was a devout man, but perhaps like many of his age, he saw religion as necessary for the poor to provide a framework for their behaviour, to prevent them sinking into a life of crime and depravity. Churches provided a centre for socialising, mutual support and education, but it seems he had no need for it. At least until he was laid in his final resting place.

Samuel kept a marble coffin in his stables at his home in London. This was unusual, as was his desire to be buried at the parish church of his country house of Wormington Grange in Gloucestershire. He left instructions for the crypt to be opened up and steps built down to it for his admission, marking him as the patron of the church. These arrangements could have been to protect his corpse from body snatching, but this seems excessive at the very least. The practice tended to serve training surgeons, the nearest of which would be in Gloucester or Bristol. It seems unlikely they would have ventured so far into the countryside.

Unlike the fashions of the time for ornately carved marble memorials, he requested a simple plaque of local bluestone with only his personal details inscribed upon it on the north wall of the chancel. His coat of arms nearby sums up the man with the motto: "RESURGAM" which means "rise" and which is open to many interpretations, such as "resist", so not all of them coffin-related. A family with his surname in Exeter suggest it was linked to the family having been bakers.

&

Most people chose to be buried in their home parish, surrounded by friends and family, but Gist was not alone. William Anderson's body was apparently placed in the crypt on his death in 1797. His classical memorial with room for his wife's details is on the chancel's south wall. Why was he not buried in his London parish either?

There is nothing to suggest Gist ever lived in his country house — he seems to have rented it out. London's churchyards were filling up at the time, which may have been a factor. Wormington Grange is now Grade II* listed, as it has fine Tudor elements, but sources claim it was built in the 1770s, and the ancient church with its curious tower was much older.

Another oddity follows from the above. Gist allocated fifty pounds to be spent planting trees for timber in the grounds of Wormington Grange, which would provide income for his cousin James Gist. This would not provide any income for many years. No mention was made of the species of tree he proposed, but the navy was a huge consumer of oak for ships, which Gist would have been well aware of. So this benefaction was not just to his heir, but to the nation and its defence, matters which were crucial to people in ports such as Bristol and London. It also fits with his favourite form of investment — government consols. In the absence of James Gist or any heirs the timber was to go to Josiah Sellick, and cascade to several others, so this bequest seems to have been important to him.

Up to his death, Gist continued to receive income from his estates spread over three counties in Virginia, and was aware of the increase in his slave population, and by the time of his death believed his proposed manumission would be accepted by the Virginia Assembly, though the large numbers of slaves involved was of concern to him. In his codicil he made allowance for the slaves in case they were not freed. He wished them to be kept together, another example of his concern for their welfare, and that more land should be purchased to keep them employed, to be paid for by the sale of government stocks. This could be read as demonstrating his miserliness, but more likely it again reflects his view that people — especially the poor — should be kept busy to prevent them falling into sloth or crime. Gist's concern for the welfare of his slaves was mentioned by the freedmen, and in his will he made a special request to his estate manager Matthew Toler "to attend to the comfort and happiness of my slaves and their issue". Fifty pounds per year was also allocated to support an Anglican cleric, and Gist also funded a school for the freedmen's children.

Gist wished every slave and their children be made free. To pay for their freedom and settling them in new homes, he bequeathed all his land, stock, tools etc, with the surplus to be divided amongst all the slaves he owned at the time of his death. The manumission was to be managed by John Wickham and Matthew Toler. This included his shares in the Great Dismal Swamp Company, and the lands purchased by Toler in the name of William Pearkes but paid for by Gist. Pearkes became Mary's second husband, which means he must also have been a citizen of North America. He was also a partner in William Anderson's tobacco importing company, but his family name can also be found in the West Country so he seems to have been yet another transatlantic businessman, perhaps also another orphan who had been sent abroad like Gist.

Regarding the land bought for Gist by Matthew Toler in the name of Mrs Pearkes but paid for by Gist, there is nothing to indicate what this land was, and this seems to be the only record of such a purchase, or even a date, which adds further confusion to the management of his will. It was probably the land purchased by her husband who demanded in his will that Gist purchase it, or return all the profits and interests he had gained from it. It seems he held it for his daughter, possibly as the executor to her late husband's will, as she could not own it in her own right. Women still became legally invisible upon marriage; they had to be represented by a male relative or representative to take action in court etc. This situation did not change until the passage of the 1884 Married Women's Property Act.

This leads to yet another aspect of Gist's benevolence. There is no mention of any plans for what he expected to happen to his freedmen. He had probably had discussed it with his agents, though not with his solicitor in Virginia. He seems to have expected his freedmen to stay on as employees, but did he investigate this before he wrote his will?

His house at Gower Street was large, so he had many staff to maintain it, yet he failed to mention any favoured domestic servants, which suggests there was no love lost between them. Or perhaps he had already made private arrangements for them before he died. He bequeathed twenty pounds to each servant who had served him for at least three years. Finally, his will provides us with the names of some of his staff. He had two clerks: George Raves, who cannot be traced, and Leighton Wood, formerly of Virginia and probably the son of the same who purchased plots of land in New Castle in 1738/9.[12] He was probably the same man or father of this name who became a major property developer in south Bristol. Though Gist's final home was a large townhouse, he only mentioned a single servant there, named Thomas Gibbons. He may have been a long term employee, and possibly the man who visited the freedmen in Brown County, as mentioned in Abdy's journal, and who had promised to help them but apparently died soon afterwards.

7

MANUMISSION

Samuel Gist is famous in the USA for having freed the greatest number of slaves, from his various plantations in Virginia. But there was a lesser-known group who were freed by an accident of history. Samuel was one of the founders of the Great Dismal Swamp Company, and he provided it with slaves to drain the swamp and cut down trees. A letter survives to Gist from his estate manager Matthew Toler informing him that during the War of Independence, most of the slaves had fled to the interior of the swamp for safety. They became the Great Dismal Swamp Maroon Settlement which provided shelter for slaves en route to freedom in the North. The population may have been as high as several thousand, and they traded with whites in the surrounding region for several generations.[1] Thus they formed a significant number of the thirty thousand that Jefferson claimed had fled the South during and after the war.

The large scale of Gist's manumission was important, as it helped set a precedent, and it allowed slaves' friends and families to remain together. Gist owned property in several counties, so when his ex-slaves were moved to their new homes, they went as a community, and were able to support and protect each other. This made logistical sense, but it also fitted with his request that they be treated kindly. Gist had a reputation for being a tough businessman, and when former neighbours from Virginia visited London, he refused to help them financially. This apparent lack of charity makes him an unlikely manumitter. Yet as his will revealed, he was active in many charities. He donated mostly to worthy causes, principally dedicated to helping the poor improve their state; he refused to provide handouts.

The most common image of the British abolition movement was produced by the potter and industrialist Josiah Wedgwood. It depicted a near-naked slave in chains, kneeling as a penitent, accompanied by the words "Am I not a Man and a Brother?" This appealed to evangelicals who saw the abolition movement as a means to promote Christianity, to increase the number of supporters of their faith, and to encourage access to the Bible which contains many stories that provide moral lessons, which encourages good citizenship. Thomas Clarkson claimed the most important element of the abolition propaganda was Charles Dibdin's play *The Padlock*, which featured a slave called Mungo — played by a white actor in apparently the first example of blackface — the forerunner of many stereotypically comical Africans. This hapless fool was promoted in the shadow of the French Revolution when poor people of every colour were feared as threats to social stability. Even promoters of education such as Hannah More and the Wesleys were seen as threats to the status quo, as French peasants were believed to have been inspired to revolt by their access to seditious literature.

Many modern authors — especially in America — question how the ludicrous Mungo could be used to represent slaves when from the outset they were known to escape whenever they could, and to withstand the most horrific punishments for even the slightest chance of freedom. From the earliest years of the terrible trade, accounts were widespread of slaves rebelling; several ships were taken over by them to return to Africa, and nets were attached to the outside of ships to catch those who preferred suicide to slavery. Early in the eighteenth century, Alexander Falconbridge, surgeon on a Bristol slave ship wrote of how slaves were constantly watching to take advantage of any negligence by their captors, and that any uprisings were generally suppressed with loss of life.[2]

In Virginia from the 1660s, slaves often joined with white indentured servants in rebellion, and in 1672 an ambitious plot by slaves alarmed a large area of Virginia. Concerns were also raised that white servants and indigenous people would join them.[3] By the end of the century the whole region had been alarmed by the prospect of violent uprisings, most of which were discovered in time to prevent them, the perpetrators tortured and/or executed.

This apparent gulf in credibility is due to the fact that many — possibly most — British abolitionists had never met a slave. Some had seen African servants, but they seemed to be treated with similar respect to Europeans, with some added curiosity. The Royal Africa Company, whose members traded with Africa, sometimes brought the sons of African leaders to Britain to entertain and educate them and to encourage trade. Missionaries sometimes converted Africans to Christianity and brought them to England to preach and encourage support for their work. Thus Britons tended to see Africans as civilised people, if curiosities.

Some people saw African musicians or preachers, and ships' officers often acquired slaves as servants in part payment after a voyage. But in 1789 *The Interesting Narrative of Olaudah Equiano* was published, the first popular account of a former slave who purchased his freedom and settled in London. His story of the horrors of his life as a slave helped fuel interest in, and support for, abolition.

Many lower class people in Britain were affected by the practice of slavery, and they knew this. Wealthy planters returned to England and bought up manors and common lands, thus depriving local people of homes and employment. Lancashire cotton factory workers were dependent on slave-produced cotton, and worked long hours in unhealthy conditions which were often compared with slavery, especially in the employment of children. Women were denied entry to universities, they were legally invisible, and when they married, their lives could be ruined by overbearing and sometimes violent husbands, so they empathised with the suffering of slaves. The poet and royal mistress Mary Robinson described herself as a bird in a gilded cage.

The English were proud of their independence, especially when compared to the alleged oppression of the Church of Rome. They could cite Magna Carta which established important rights for all, and which formed the basis for many constitutions, including that of the USA. It was cited when abolitionists attempted to free slaves who landed on British soil. Some people believed that Christian baptism or marriage granted them freedom. Christianity itself had been born out of slavery, so it seems peculiar that so many people claiming to be pious could have clear consciences about enslaving others.

The English were very late arrivals to the business of slavery which had long been the realm of the Catholics of Spain and Portugal who were seen as still living in the darkness of the unre-formed church. Whilst these nations were importing huge amounts of gold and silver into Europe, which introduced inflation, the English were too busy fighting amongst themselves to build overseas empires. The Dutch colonised Brazil where they discovered how to grow and process sugar cane, which led the English to realise it was a source of great wealth. It was more labour-intensive than tobacco, so they began planting it in their West Indies colonies, launching the nation into the African slave trade. They began with Barbados, which was largely worked by indentured or kidnapped Britons, but when Cromwell took Jamaica from the Spanish in the mid seven-teenth century, the trickle of West Indian gold turned into a flood.

The English revulsion at Catholic practices and slavery shifted at the Restoration in 1660; Charles II had lived in Catholic Europe where he enjoyed opulent living, and encouraged a shift in trade towards high-profit colonial produce. He licensed the Royal Africa Company to trade British goods for gold on Africa's west coast in 1672; the following year, slave trading began. In the 1680s Africans were sent to South Carolina as they had knowledge of growing rice. But slave trading was never fully embraced.

As early as 1679 the Habeas Corpus Act was passed which meant no subject of the realm could be sent abroad as a prisoner; this was probably a response to the spiriting away of English people, but it had implications for slaves brought to these shores. In 1696 because laws in the colonies differed from those of Britain, so challenges were brought. Common law did not recognise Africans as being different to Europeans. Yet they could be bought and sold as chattels in Barbados, though this was not legal in Britain. A slave who arrived in Britain could be a *villein* but not a *slave*.[4] Hence, the rights to own slaves was disputed from the outset. But the huge distances between London's legal institutions and the colonies, together with the huge profits to be made from trading in humans, led to these rights being ignored for decades.

Growing evidence suggests people of colour have lived in the British Isles for centuries; they were here in Roman times, and the base of Nelson's Column shows African sailors serving in the navy. As in the early plantations, black and white sailors worked alongside each other, and their lives were often mutually dependent to survive the many dangers at sea. After the passage of the Abolition of the Slave Trade Act, the navy was active in policing the trade. Many sailors took huge risks, even breaking international law to pursue slave ships, which suggests how important the cause was to them.

When Woodes Rogers made his famous voyage from Bristol, he recorded a crew numbering only two hundred and twenty-five, of whom only about forty were sailors. Over a third were foreign, the rest included peddlers and fiddlers.[5] How did such a motley crew ever get clear of port, never mind survive thousands of miles at sea and to win battles against foreign ships? Their achievements were truly mind-boggling. During long journeys, men died, fell ill, were injured, and often absconded in port, so Britain's maritime and merchant ships were heavily dependent on foreigners, some of whom came from Africa.

Africans were often noted as servants, leading some historians to claim there was a significant population in Britain. But this does not mean they had children. Sailors were highly mobile, so may have left 'a child in every port', though high infant mortality probably meant few reached adulthood. Servants were generally young people saving to marry, or else they remained single for life, so many black servants may also have left no descendants.

Slavery was often justified by slave owners on the grounds that slaves had no feelings. But this makes no sense as families were often separated to prevent rebellions. The tearing apart of slave families was often condemned as the worst of the many abuses committed by slave traders, as the Romantic Movement in Britain increasingly emphasised the importance of family bonds, especially that between mothers and children.

Bacon's Rebellion in Virginia in 1676, which united slaves, servants and free settlers, came dangerously close to overthrowing the colony's government. It highlighted the lack of a sizeable middle class who could suppress such uprisings and also defend against foreign invasion. This led to the separation of African slaves from European servants. African slaves were banned from owning property, dogs or firearms, running a business or taking legal action. If they were attacked by a white man, they could not retaliate, not even to save their own life.[6]

As recently as 1788 a white man killing a slave was not a crime, while in Britain stealing a lamb or a fish and petty acts of vandalism were capitol offences under Walpole's Black Acts. As late as 1847 — over two decades after Britain's Great Reform Act — slaves were still not covered by common law or Magna Carta which protected everyone in Britain. Some justified this on the bizarre grounds that they "the evils of American slavery are blessings as compared with the general fate of the African race in their native continent".[7]

By the outbreak of the War of Independence, increasing numbers of slaves were acquiring skills to make up the shortfall of white immigrants. The war highlighted the dangers of the colonies' dependence on imports. This inspired the establishment of local industries, which often relied on skilled workers, some of whom were slaves. But slaves undermined the wages of free workers, producing one of the many threads of racism. In the USA, abolition pitched two groups against each other: the plantocracy with their huge estates based on slave labour and growing numbers of poor and middle class immigrants such as the Scottish Presbyterians, German Lutherans and Irish Protestants who complained that slavery discouraged white immigration and the establishment of civil society This claim was even made in Virginia, where slavery was blamed for holding back industries and discouraging young immigrants. Black sailors had often filled gaps in British crews, described by one source as: "great, handsome, muscular fellows, invaluable on shipboard."[8] But in North America, laws were passed restricting the numbers of slaves in the maritime trades.[9]

By the 1770s immigrants to Virginia were of increasing variety. A ship arrived in Norfolk with forty tradesmen, indentured for only four years, so they must have been supplying a known need. They were noted as being blacksmiths, carpenters, tailors, weavers etc.[10] Three years later a shipment brought a plasterer, barber, staymaker, printer, bookbinder, stocking weaver, silk dyer, schoolmaster and hatter,[11] so colonial culture was catching up with Europe. Over the same period, convicts and slaves were still being shipped, suggesting a chaotic influx of people in the run up to the war.

English law is a complicated beast. Unlike in the post-revolutionary countries of the USA and France, it has never been codified. It resembles some of the earliest computer programs that have been repeatedly updated and modified, but the system cannot be paused to allow it to be rewritten or overhauled. It is too big and would be far too expensive to be updated to modern standards. If an action had been practised "time out of mind", i.e. beyond the memory of the oldest in a community, it was generally accepted as being legal. No law was ever passed in England which made slavery legal, and

Magna Carta still held. But whilst it soon became essential in the West Indies to replace indentured servants and the poor; in Virginia, it evolved to replace indentured servants and criminals. Planters of the West Indies produced so much wealth they became a significant lobby group; they spent huge sums buying seats in parliament to promote their own interests, and most of Britain's wars in the eighteenth century were fought to protect them.

But when these wealthy planters returned to Britain — either for their health or for business or family reasons — they often brought with them their personal slaves, which some sources claimed to number in the tens of thousands, though this was probably an exaggeration. This created a huge problem for the legal system, as slavery was legal in the colonies, but not in Britain. Slaves were seen as a threat to English liberty. Some opponents of the institution believed that a slave became free when they set foot on English soil, as they were covered by English common law. But if so, they could not be returned to the plantations, and when slave owners came to Britain, they would not be able to bring their slaves with them. Sugar plantations were highly profitable, so still needed a large slave force to work them. If such freedom was accepted, it was seen as a forerunner to the abolition of the trade in humans, which, it was feared, could trigger a major financial crisis by making the West Indies plantations worthless.

In 1771 the matter came to a head when a slave called James Somerset was baptised in London and escaped from his master. When recaptured by his master, his godparents appealed to Lord Mansfield for a writ of habeas corpus which forced his captors to present him to court and explain the reason for his detention. It was fortunate that Lord Mansfield was the judge, as he had adopted two nieces, one of whom was the child of his brother, a naval officer and a female slave. This made Mansfield sympathetic to the rights of slaves, but he was part of the establishment, so was unlikely to threaten the nation's economy.

The Somerset case became a cause célèbre, as it provided a chance to clarify the legal status of slaves, and threatened to establish dangerous precedents with both sides predicting apocalypse if they lost. Somerset eventually won his case on the grounds that he had been kidnapped, which was a crime in Britain. In effect, he had freed himself, which conveniently failed to create a precedent, and passed the debate to the public realm, beyond the remit of a single law maker.

During the War of Independence, the Governor of Virginia Lord Dunmore offered freedom to any slaves who fled to support Britain. But this only applied to men willing to carry arms and if their master was not a loyalist. Thus, this was a matter of military expediency rather than a precedent or change of national policy. But Cornwallis's recruitment of former slaves was seen by colonists as inflammatory by arming slaves in a colony so often beset by rebellions. The war moved from being one of independence from taxation to a battle for slavery as well. In 1775 three hundred escaped slaves joined the Ethiopian Regiment; the following year, the Black Pioneers Regiment was created.[12] But at the disastrous Siege of Yorktown, when Dunmore's troops were forced to eat their own horses, the freedmen were abandoned: either as victims in battle or to return to slavery.

At the end of the war, land was granted to black war veterans in Nova Scotia, but the best land was allocated to white settlers. Some ex-slaves were sent to New York before it fell, but were still at risk of capture there. When the British finally left, these freed slaves were taken to London, where their safety was ensured. But that was their sole reward. They were foreign-born, and mostly unemployed, so under the Poor Laws, no parish was responsible for their care. The capital thus had two types of Africans: well dressed and well fed slaves, and the ragged war veterans who starved on the streets, especially in the notorious slum of Seven Dials. As was so common with the British, there is no sign of any overall plan for them. No provision had been made for them on their arrival, and after the war many unemployed British poor flocked to the cities in search of work, so their suffering was part of the usual downturn in the post-war economy.

Thus, the situation echoed the problems of Tudor times, with the streets full of homeless poor, but their colour made them stand out, and they were a constant reminder of British betrayal and broken promises. Concerns were raised that they would marry white women, again, a product of post-war times when there was a huge shortage of eligible men, but also raising fears of them weakening the white English population. At the same time, the loss of the American colonies meant there was nowhere to dump the criminal — or rather, criminalised — poor, so there were concerns about the rising numbers detained on the hulks on the Thames. Proud English citizens were offended by the sight of their countrymen in chains, so an alternative location was desperately sought for them.

The winter of 1785/6 was colder than usual, so attention was drawn to the veterans suffering and sometimes dying on public streets. A Committee for the Relief of the Black Poor was established in Batson's Coffee Shop opposite the Exchange.[13] Gist must have known of this, and possibly donated to it, along with other loyalist traders. A major donor was John Julius Angerstein, an insurance underwriter and founder of the New Lloyds coffee house and whose art collection formed the basis of the National Gallery. The bulk of funds came from the government, as the men were ultimately their responsibility. Food, clothing and survival funds were provided, but this was only a short-term fix. It became clear to many that there was no long term future for them in England. A decision was made to send the former slaves "back" to Africa, to a home most of them had never known.

In the mistaken belief that the west coast of Africa had fertile soil and moderate weather, plans were begun to found the colony of Sierra Leone. Three ships sailed in January 1787, organised by Granville Sharp who had supported Somerset and other freed slaves. He proposed the new, utopian settlement follow the archaic Anglo-Saxon law of Frankpledge under which all members of the community collaborated.[14] It is unclear why Sharpe chose this system; did he see the new land as a form of utopia which required utopian laws? The system could not have worked as a British governor was in charge, and the territory was expected to trade with

Britain, to exchange local goods for manufactured imports. Slavery was banned, though the major slave centre of Bunce Island was only a few miles away; so the new settlers could see the ships sailing past with their captives, which cannot have made them feel safe. Worst of all, the organisers had been misinformed. The young settlement's crops were washed away soon after they were planted, storms battered their farms, and the area became covered in stagnant water to breed diseases such as malaria and dysentery.

But Sharpe refused to concede defeat. Thomas Clarkson's brother, the naval officer John was put in charge of a second flotilla of fifteen ships which sailed from Halifax, Nova Scotia in January 1792. They eventually established a settlement that became the capital of Sierra Leone, Freetown. In 1800 the Maroons of Jamaica rebelled and were deported there, so the colony became a place of exile and punishment. But it has survived to become the oldest black democracy in Africa, and where women were allowed to vote for public office, over a century before this was achieved in Britain. The governor who followed Clarkson was William Dawes, an officer in the first fleet that founded the colony of Botany Bay in the future Australia.[15] In the wake of Britain's ban on the slave trade in 1807, the Royal Navy patrolled the west coast of Africa, capturing slave ships and their human cargo, and Freetown became their base.

When the British government considered plans to end the African slave trade, investigations were made into two possible outcomes. The authorities feared that abolition would lead to former slaves ceasing to work, being too lazy or ignorant to support themselves, echoing their views about the British and Irish poor. But following the revolution in Haiti — which some Members of Parliament had witnessed as army officers — there was also widespread concern that if the slaves were not freed, the alternative would be widespread bloodshed and destruction of property. Ultimately, the decision was probably made on financial grounds, caused by the decline in fertility of the soil in the West Indies, so crops such as sugar declined. Napoleonic France grew sugar beet, which was cheaper than the Caribbean crop, undermining the trade. Since Gist was a businessman, economics must have played a significant role in his decision. It seems the soil of the old plantations was no longer supporting tobacco and poor Europeans were emigrating in large numbers, so slavery was becoming less necessary to the point of redundancy. Timing was thus crucial, as slavery didn't die out in America. It was merely moribund.[16]

Southern colonies produced exotic crops such as indigo, rice, and especially tobacco. But in Europe the demand for tobacco stagnated, in part due to the rise in genteel entertainments such as assembly rooms, which became popular at the expense of smoke-filled coffee houses and inns. Prices of crops varied, and when high yields threatened, planters burned crops in the fields to keep profits high.[17] This made land available for other crops so many planters turned to cotton for which there was a huge demand in Britain's factories. But the plant produced seeds which were difficult to remove by hand, a matter that had led to the decline in the trade in India. The problem was solved by Eli Whitney, a graduate of Yale with an interest in mechanics who invented the first cotton gin in 1792. A metal roller picked up the cotton and carried it to a metal grill where the seeds were scraped away. Hogden Holmes improved it to allow a single slave to do the work of twelve hand workers. It was improved again on large plantations to be driven by a water-wheel, further increasing efficiency. His invention was described as "the making of the South".[18]

Manumission was not unknown in the slave colonies; owners sometimes purchased freedom for a favoured servant by deed or included it in their will. But this was mostly for house slaves, who lived in close contact with families and were similar to domestic servants in Europe. They were treated much better than the many field slaves, so were less likely to rebel or try to escape. Deeds were used to free slaves faster, and were often the choice of those opposed to slavery, such as Quakers who banned their members from slave trading in 1761. But these deeds were frequently made by people with smaller numbers of slaves, and they often only freed a few of them. Some families had only four or five slaves; they all worked together in the fields; they knew and respected each other, so the masters were more likely to free such a slave as reward for loyalty and/or hard work. Since it was made during the master's lifetime, the deed was less likely to be challenged, and any problems such as opposition by the colony's assembly could be dealt with promptly.

Wills tended to be used to free larger numbers of slaves, often by people with fewer heirs. But as the former owner was dead, these could be challenged. In 1827 John Nelson jun. of Mecklenburg County requested an act to allow a slave called Corban to remain in the Commonwealth of Virginia, despite being emancipated by his late father.[19] This seems to show a disregard for the wishes of his late father, as well as contempt for the welfare of a valued servant. But perhaps Nelson was concerned as to how the former slave would survive in a Slave State. His servant may even have requested the son's petition, as he may not have wished to leave his home, friends and family.

Some historians have complained of the patriarchal attitude shown by the various authorities towards Gist's slaves, of the close supervision and failure to listen to their concerns, all of which were probably true. But the process of manumission was overseen by the Court of Chancery, which dealt with inheritances, so conservative behaviour was its defining characteristic. It protected heirs who were often women and children, who had no legal status, as was the situation with the slaves. Every action and item of expenditure had to be recorded and legally defensible, leaving little room for initiative or to comply with the needs or requests of those in their care.

Accusations of paternalism also tend to ignore the many problems the freedmen faced. They may have spent their entire lives working on a plantation, having all their food and accommodation supplied. Gist still sent them clothes and blankets after he returned to England, so they may have suffered in the outside world. People who have spent long periods in institutions such as hospitals or prisons and even the military often struggle to cope outside them. The freedmen may never have learned to manage their own lives. It is unclear how Gist's former slaves engaged with the wider world, and how much supervision and support they received whilst waiting for their fates to be settled.

Even if they were successful at surviving life beyond their plantations, they were still legally invisible. Even the most intelligent, hard working and worldly-wise freedman would be vulnerable to white people exploiting and abusing them, as was described to Rev. Abdy when he visited the settlements in 1833/4. He was told how hard it was for the settlement people to find work, how they were underpaid or not paid at all, and that the agents who were supposed to provide support often defrauded them of what they believed to be their dues. They were unable to defend themselves in court or take action against anyone who mistreated or harmed them. Gist was probably aware of this in making allowances for them to be educated. If they were able to read, they could at least understand legal documents which they might have needed to sign. As the settlements struggled, suggestions were made that there should be schools taught by white people to help protect them, which seems to confirm this.

In 1723 Virginia banned manumission, but by the 1770s the cause of abolition was on the rise in Britain, and in North America many slave owners — especially Quakers — were freeing their slaves with impunity. But these were in small numbers, so the legislature apparently overlooked them. In 1782 this restriction was repealed on condition the freedmen paid their taxes and the owner guaranteed that they would never be in need of charity. This shows the opposition to their freedom continued to be based on their perceived laziness, and in later years the same terms were applied when Irish servants were sent to the colony.

Quakers were active campaigners for emancipation and in Virginia in 1782 an act was passed to authorise manumission, though it was still restricted. Local courts decided whether the slaves were sound in body and mind, and they had to be younger than forty-five years of age, and men had to be over twenty-one and women eighteen. They also needed to be "supported and maintained by, the person so liberating them, or by his or her estate".[20] The act was so popular that within two years of its passage, the population of free negroes had doubled. Many people thus believed slavery was heading for extinction. The Virginian authorities were even making plans for this in 1777, but the tide turned, and in 1785 a petition supported by Methodists and Baptists for abolition of the trade was opposed.

The uprisings in Haiti of the 1790s sent shockwaves through the Slave States. But these events were far from typical. The slaves had been freed by the French in the spirit of revolutionary egalitarianism, but then re-enslaved when Caribbean produce was needed to fund France's ongoing wars against the British. In Virginia, restrictions were re-introduced in 1793 and free blacks were banned from entering the state. In 1800 the Gabriel Insurrection in Richmond brought all the slave owners' nightmares into sharp reality, triggering more debates on restrictive laws against slaves and freedmen.

Large-scale manumission also created new problems, as single slaves could easily integrate into white society, while a large group could not. This meant that land had to be found for them to settle, either in America, or Africa. In the wake of the Napoleonic Wars and the War of 1812, Europe was awash with unemployed people, and England's overseers of the poor were still offering their charges for work in industries, so plentiful cheap labour was arriving in North America for free. Had Britain not lost the War of Independence, the country would have continued exporting their poor and prisoners, who were often the same, so the demand for slaves would have fallen sooner. Profits from tobacco production in the Tidewater region were falling due to the need to fertilise the soil, which led to a fall in demand for slave labour. But Europe's rising population created new demands for food, so land was increasingly used to grow corn in Virginia, and rice in South Carolina.

The first Gist freedman settlements were in Brown County, near the farms of Quakers so there should have been little resistance to them. But they were also on the main route of the Underground Railroad, so runaway slaves were drawn to their settlement and some of the freedmen were actively involved in helping them. This in turn put them at risk from the many slave catchers who crossed from the southern Slave States and acted with impunity. Even though Ohio did not allow slavery, it did not prosecute those in search of runaways, who sometimes took freedmen. It seems a member of the Underground Railroad, John Mahan, prevented Eliza Johnson being returned to slavery.[21] But due to the freemen not leaving any written records, and the under-reporting of non-whites in mainstream records, there were probably plenty of other near misses or worse.

Some slaves who were granted freedom applied to stay in Virginia and in 1815 an act was passed to allow freed slaves of exceptional character to remain. Nancy, who was freed by the will of her former master John A Binns, applied to stay in Virginia in 1815, and Nathan who had been freed by his master the late Edward Brown asked for permission to remain in 1830.[22]

Such requests seem to make no sense: surely every slave would welcome freedom. But this is to ignore the many problems faced by freed slaves, especially if they were on their own. Some preferred to remain because they had friends or family who they did not want to be parted from. Field slaves were probably less skilled, so less likely to thrive when freed, but they may also have been less likely to be freed by their masters. House — or body — slaves could probably find employment; they spent much of their lives in the company of their masters and mistresses so understood the workings of white society.

In Britain, skilled domestic servants could save enough money to set up in business on their own, running coffee shops and pubs, often with the financial backing and support of their former masters. This may have been possible for freed slaves. Some male slaves learned much-needed trades, becoming blacksmiths and carpenters. They may have fared better as the colonies expanded their towns and industries, especially following the Revolutionary War. The most successful of these was John P. Parker, a slave whose father was white, and who was sold into slavery at the age of eight. He learned to read and write, worked hard and bought his own freedom at the age of eighteen. He became an inventor and mechanic and moved to Ripley, where he played an active role in not just hiding fleeing slaves, but crossing the Ohio River to Kentucky to guide them to safety.[23]

Slaves were treated as chattels to be bought and sold, but they were still humans who formed relationships and produced children. When a white couple married, they could each bring slaves to the marriage, some of whom formed relationships, so if one of the owners died, who owned the slave children? George Washington wished to free his slaves, as in the Roman practice, at his death. He believed slavery should not be for life, and that loyalty and hard work should be rewarded. But his widow still needed an income, so he requested they be freed when Martha died. Gist allowed several options if his proposed manumission was not possible, one of which was that the slaves should be kept together to provide income for his two daughters.

When David Anderson — father of Gist's son- in-law William — wrote his will in 1793, he requested his slaves be distributed among his many children and grandchildren. He gave his son Nathaniel several slaves including Frances, but not her daughter, who was granted to his granddaughters. Likewise, his son Richard Anderson was granted Easther whose daughter of the same name was also left to them, suggesting slaves were passed on to heirs of similar age.[24] It seems cruel to separate families but he must have been referring to house slaves, or perhaps companions to the daughters before they were old enough to do hard manual work. In the survey of Gist's lands of 1783, two plantations in Goochland had only sixteen slaves, and another had thirty-one. In Hanover County, Woodberry had twenty-three and Dundee which became home to his son-in-law William Anderson, was by far the largest with forty-eight. A further fifteen slaves were with Mr Anderson — probably William again — but their location is unrecorded. About half this population were children, which explains why there was such an increase in their numbers in the ensuing decades. Again, this raises questions as to the viability of the practice of slavery in Virginia, as

Anderson had many relatives to whom he could have bequeathed them.

&

The freeing of Gist's slaves may also have been a means of unravelling some convoluted threads of inheritance. He was executor of the wills of his former master John Smith, and of Smith's uncle John Massie, both of whom passed slaves on to their heirs on various terms, not all of which are clear. Gist was guardian to Smith's two sons and heirs, and on their deaths, he inherited all their estates which included the above two. Gist also inherited his wife's dowry and any family legacies. When Gist's son-in-law William Anderson died, he became his heir, which brought him yet more land and slaves.

Following two centuries of social and political chaos, Britain in the late seventeenth century was beginning to emerge from the darkness. It needed a model for a new democracy and turned to the ancient world, especially Rome, which became a popular destination for young men finishing their educations on the Grand Tour. England only had two universities, mostly for training clerics, physicians and lawmakers, so travel to Europe was a means of widening their horizons. Slavery had been widespread in the ancient world, as a means of employing prisoners of war, and who provided the empire with cheap labour. This is yet another aspect of the African slave trade which is overlooked. Europeans did not capture slaves; they purchased them as prisoners of war, so for many decades Africans were treated as white political prisoners, and would have been subject to extreme punishment if they misbehaved. But the fall in the supply of European slave labour led to a rise in the use of Africans. They were traded for guns and ammunition, which gave their sellers an advantage in battles, fuelling the capture of enemies to be sold into slavery.

But Roman slavery was not for life; slaves were generally from areas within the empire, so they could become free and return home at the end of their service. They were also provided with the means of advancement, and could become citizens and even own their own slaves. It is unknown how widespread manumission was: it probably depended on the demand for labour at the time. Livy wrote that Rome passed a law in 357 B.C. called Rex Mania, imposing a tax on any new manumissions.[25] After the disaster at Cannae, Rome suffered a huge manpower shortage so in order to rebuilt the city, the empire recruited an army of slaves who would be freed after three years.[26]

Roman slavery and manumissions did not involve any moral considerations. Unlike in the New World, slaves were considered to have free will but were still inclined to be lazy. But talented slaves were sometimes offered the chance of freedom which inspired them to work harder, with manumission as their reward. The slave population of the New World steadily increased as land was cleared and planted, but in Rome, slave numbers varied in response to demand, and as battles were won, and as slaves obtained their freedom

.Slaves in Rome were often freed on the death of their masters, as a reward for years of loyalty. Those who showed initiative and hard work could learnt trades, and could purchase their own freedom and even own slaves themselves, a practice occasionally possible in the early North American colonies, and a few earned enough to free themselves.

The English and Americans modelled themselves on the democratic state of Rome, so it is not surprising that statesman and soldier George Washington wished to free his slaves on his death. This is possibly why his sometime business partner Samuel Gist wished to emancipate his slaves, to demonstrate his enlightenment. He had probably learned at least the basics of a classical education at Queen Elizabeth's Hospital. The status of mixed-race people was also not fixed, especially when wealth was involved. The Piercefield estate near Chepstow on the border of Wales was purchased in 1802 by Nathaniel Wells. He was born in St Kitts, son of William Wells, a former Cardiff sugar baker and his house slave, Juggy. He became hugely wealthy and married the daughter of the former chaplain to the king. He was the richest person of mixed race of the time, and became Sheriff of Monmouth in 1818, the first person of mixed race to hold such an office in Britain. He owned slaves and for a time this included his own mother.[27]

Gist's decision to free his slaves was easier as an absentee owner. He did not have to live with the fallout of his decision. Slavery in the New World was far more pernicious than the Roman model as it was not only lifelong, but also became hereditary. In Rome there was a uniting sense of promoting the civilising role of the empire, offering slaves hope of a better future for themselves and their families, whereas on plantations the aim was purely to make money for the owners. Slaves were often encouraged to have children who could be put to work or sold for profit. This system provided no hope of escape or redemption, and life without hope is not a life at all.

We have no idea if Gist had any choice in his own emigration to Virginia, but he seemed to have left as soon as he was free of his legal commitments. He claimed he was in poor health, but he survived into his tenth decade, which makes this unlikely. But his two stepsons —like many other Virginians — died young, probably as the low lying land of the Tidewater region was a fertile breeding ground for mosquitoes and the diseases they spread such as malaria. Gist left his wife behind, which seems cruel and adds to his reputation of being mercenary. But perhaps this was her choice. She may have already been ill, and/or was unwilling to leave her friends and family, though their daughters were keen to sail to a new life in the bustling metropolis of London. Perhaps their marriage was — like so many — one based on survival and economic necessity, which meant there were few tears shed when they separated.

8

_____

ENACTING GIST'S WILL

B y the time Samuel Gist wrote his will in London in 1808, he
had been away from Virginia for four decades. In the
interim, the War of Independence had been fought to a
stalemate, and by the time Gist died in 1815, the two nations were
again fighting each other. The legal and social landscape of the
former colony had radically changed as the laws of Britain were
being rewritten by and for the use of the new nation.

That was the start of his problems. The United States was no
longer a British colony; its people no longer saw Britons as their
masters or betters. Most of the people Gist had known were dead,
so there were few people with any ties of friendship to be motivated
carry out the instructions of his will. At best he would have been
seen as a distant figure; at worst, he was a traitor who exploited
people and in some instances had pursued even small debts with a
determination that seemed beyond reason.

He appointed the famous loyalist lawyer John Wickham (1763–
1839) to carry out his will, but this was without any prior consulta-
tion or consent. Wickham had pursued colonial debts on behalf of
Gist and other loyalists, and navigated the passage of Samuel's will
through the High Court in Virginia to ensure its legality. But he

refused any further involvement, probably aware of the difficulties that lay ahead. He handed the responsibilities to his son William Fanning Wickham (1793–1880), a graduate of Princeton, who worked with the Court of Chancery to fulfil Gist's intentions as closely as possible. He spent vast amounts of time and effort investigating various possibilities, including whether Sierra Leone would be the most suitable option. He became responsible for preparing the slaves for their move, with tasks such as purchasing their certificates of manumission, clothes and tools, arranging transport, buying new land for them and disposing of the Virginia plantations.

Gist had hoped his estate manager Matthew Toler or his heirs would ensure the practicalities ran smoothly. Toler was married to a slave, so his four children were of mixed race. But Toler had recently died, a huge loss to the cause, as he had a personal interest in their success. Some of the descendants of the original freemen have his surname, so are probably descended from him. He could also have chosen to live with them which may have provided them with much needed protection and advice.

Gist's will was huge: eighteen pages of closely written and amended pages of parchment which became fifty-eight pages when copied for North American use. This seems an incredible amount of detail, but reflects the situation in Britain following the English Civil War when the ecclesiastical courts which dealt with inheritances and family matters collapsed. The courts struggled to recover, as many people abandoned the Church of England for the many Nonconformist groups. By the middle of the eighteenth century, the economy was booming, so more people were affluent enough to justify the cost of writing wills to pass on their estates when they died. But the courts failed to cope with the extra workload, resulting in huge delays in the settlement of estates, so many beneficiaries died before they received their dues. To avoid entering into this black hole, people wrote long, detailed wills which allowed for all conceivable contingencies, so property and goods could be passed on to various male or female heirs.

A major change which had a huge impact on Gist's legacy was the passage of a law in 1806 which forced slaves to leave Virginia within a year of their emancipation or they would be re-enslaved. This was a revival of an act of 1691. Gist's will stated that his lands should be sold within a year to pay for his slaves to be moved, which suggests he knew of this new law. But part of the legacy was to be paid for by the tobacco crops, which were harvested in autumn. This allowed the slaves' manumission when the money he allocated was at its maximum. He may have feared they would stop working once freed, which would deplete the funds he had allocated. The freedmen could have the winter to resettle, then start their lives afresh. If the manumission was not possible, he wished his slaves to continue working his land, with the profits going to his daughters for the remainder of their lives.

But the law can be a curious beast. Just because it exists doesn't mean that it is always enforced. In 1815 an act was passed modifying this law which allowed slaves of 'good character' or 'extraordinary merit'

to remain in the state. This seems to have again echoed the fears of them failing to support themselves. After 1816 this was expanded to county and city courts, but many applications were denied.

Without investigating a single instance, the legislature made it clear that remaining in the state was not an option for any of the Gist slaves,[1] so we have no idea if any of them demonstrated the valuable skills and respectable behaviour which would have allowed them to stay. But this may have had little impact as the slaves seem to have had close-knit families, so would have wished to stay together.

Wickham purchased three hundred and fifty certificates of emancipation in 1818, already an increase from Gist's estimate of two hundred and seventy five. This shows the number of slaves in his charge at the time, and indicated his intention to begin transporting them to new land in Ohio. But their removal was repeatedly delayed. Technically, they could have been re-enslaved, but there is no suggestion that this was ever considered by the legislature. The last of them did not leave till 1831, leaving behind five who were too elderly and infirm to survive the long journey, as Gist had made allowances for.

Gist believed he had left more than enough for them to live in comfort. But this was based on them remaining in the state, so there were no funds for their relocation. He also failed to allow for the costs and delays caused by challenges to his will, which he must have at least suspected given the problems with his land purchases, and should have resolved long before he died. The most important of these came from the descendants of William Anderson, the late husband of Gist's daughter Mary.

Gist left Virginia in 1765, before the outbreak of the War of Independence. But this left his property at risk of sequestration, as he was declared to be an enemy. Gist's eldest daughter, Mary, was married to William Anderson, a member of the Virginia Assembly; he became the commissioner for Gist's lands in 1778. To further protect the properties, in 1782 he arranged for an act to be passed which vested the lands with Mary — as a native of Virginia — in perpetuity.[2] This act was clear that these lands were for her and her heirs to own, but Gist claimed this was never his intention. Yet when Gist later demanded the return of his lands and slaves, he was forced to buy them for ten thousand pounds plus five hundred pounds per year in interest.[3] To complicate matters further, he instructed Anderson to buy two properties on his behalf, and throughout the war he received the profits from them. But he failed to reimburse Anderson's costs. So in Anderson's will, he left the land to Gist on condition that these debts were cleared within a year of his own death. But it seems Wickham knew nothing of this problem, as he sold the land for seventeen thousand dollars as part of Gist's estate.[4] This oversight created the biggest of many headaches for Wickham, as Anderson's heirs challenged and delayed the settlement of Gist's will until the matter was settled for fifty thousand dollars.[5]

The transfer of property suggests Gist was trying to cheat the system and/or his daughter and son-in-law; but if he was, he was far from alone. When war broke out, many loyalists tried to remove or protect their properties before fleeing to Britain. More likely, Gist was trying to cling to his property at a time of chaos, when fixed laws were becoming flexible; like so many at the time he was trying to run a business built on quicksand on both sides of the Atlantic. It was a very big, complex omelette he was trying to make, and lots of eggs were inevitably broken in the process.

Perhaps when he wrote his will he assumed his good intentions towards the slaves would prevent any challenges to it. Or perhaps his failing memory had caused him to forget the many loose ends he had left during his empire building. Some sources claim his daughters and their husbands challenged the will in Virginia on the basis that it was unfair to them to be left only five hundred pounds per year. But this is not the case. The Andersons and the Fowkes approved of the manumission and surrendered any claims to Gist's Virginia estates. They had all benefited from Gist's wealth throughout their lives, both men had their own businesses, and they were provided with sizeable legacies based on Gist's English estates. They had no need to refuse the slaves their legacies, and probably discussed his proposals and agreed with them before he died.

There were also two suits, the details of which are lost, which were fought out in Britain's High Court of Chancery and concerned the five thousand pounds plus interest which had been left to Gist's heirs who were alive at his death.

Another suit was brought by Thomas Reade Rootes jun. He was the step son of Joseph Smith, Gist's late step son. When Gist's wife Mary Smith's previous husband John Smith died, he made Gist guardian to his sons John jun. and Joseph, the latter of whom became the second husband of Sarah Reade Rootes, whose only child was the challenger. Reade Rootes jun. studied at William and Mary College and on his graduation became a prominent lawyer, possibly inspired by his desire to inherit his various families' wealth. He sought advice from Patrick Henry, but the latter became too busy to pursue the matter on his behalf.[6] Gist had previously sought advice from Charles Yorke, the future Lord Chancellor of England regarding his own earlier dispute with his stepson, the late Joseph Smith.[7]

But Reade Rootes abandoned his claim in 1822 and died in January 1824, which put an apparent end to the family's convoluted claim on Gist's estate. It is possible it would have failed anyway, due to the length of time that had elapsed and Gist's claims that most of the relevant documents had been lost. But these proceedings added delays to the freeing of the slaves in case funds needed to be paid out in settlement. There were also debts to be collected via courts, with the estate of someone called Campbell paying a debt of five thousand dollars.[8] Gist's shares in the Great Dismal Swamp Company had been sold for ten thousand dollars in 1818.[9]

These demands on Gist's estate were all in breach of his wishes, as he stated that any American debts were to be paid out of his huge British wealth. Wickham had made enquiries of a solicitor in London who advised him the claim was unlikely to succeed.[10] This seems to have been poor advice, as the will had been proven in England. But it would have taken so much time and expense in the Court of Chancery that the slaves might never have been freed. This seems to have been the source of the many rumours that have circulated in the intervening years, that various Britons — including the government — had stolen or withheld funds. Nothing was stolen: the creaking machinery of British justice simply made claims against Gist's English estate unfeasible. If anyone was to blame, it was Gist for not doing his research before writing his will. But he was an old man when he died, so cannot be expected to be at his best. Allowances must also be made for the huge changes that had occurred throughout his life: financial, legal and social, all of which had an impact on this story.

The scale of Gist's plan was unprecedented, and Wickham struggled to obtain advice on how best to proceed. The situation was further complicated by the timing: post war, there was high unemployment and the economy was depressed. The War of 1812 evolved from a maritime trade dispute between Napoleon and Britain which caused a fall in US trade. When a British ship sent a press gang to take some US sailors at sea, the former colony was drawn into the dispute. Allegations were made that the British supported indigenous people, which restricted the expansion of settlements, so war broke out. The young nation's capital of Washington was sacked and the White House burned; it acquired its name when it was later whitewashed to cover the damage. US military victories encouraged the nascent country, while the British embargo further encouraged the Americans to develop their own industries.[11] Thus, Gist's manumission was begun at the worst possible time, potentially causing opposition to be raised against it on the basis of his nationality, to be added to any racist or procedural reasons.

The executors sought advice from Captain Paul Cuffe (1759–1817), an Episcopalian minister of New England, who built a shipping empire even though he was of mixed race.[12] Like the Virginia Assembly, he supported the removal of freed slaves to found colonies in Africa. Following the War of Independence he had helped the British resettlement of freed slaves to Nova Scotia and Sierra Leone. But the latter was struggling, so, as Haiti welcomed settlers, this was also considered.

The Pennsylvania Abolition Society eventually put Wickham in contact with Quakers to act as agents in Ohio. The most important member was storekeeper Joshua Woodrow in Hillsboro, Highland County, whose family were active in local commerce and industry. Levi Warner was originally from Pennsylvania; he raised cattle which he drove to Philadelphia, so he had commercial contacts there. Unusually for a Quaker he also managed a tavern.[13] Enoch Lewis was from Virginia and settled in Highland County about 1829[14] so was the closest to the settlements and was involved in the later management rather than the founding of the settlements. His farm was a station on the Underground Railroad.[15]

Further delays were caused by the difficulty in finding enough land for such a large group. Even in Free States such as Ohio, few white settlers would welcome a large settlement of black people as neighbours. Concerns were raised of settlements being too close to the river, putting them at risk of slave catchers, but placing them further north meant the land was of poorer quality, so Wickham was warned of possible problems.[16]

In the early years of the century, opposition to manumission led to increasing support for returning freed slaves to Africa. Charities were formed by Granville Sharp in England to settle Sierra Leone. The Royal Navy approved the settlement, and the British Treasury approved funds of fourteen pounds per person for clothes and medicine, and provided three months' food which was how long they naively believed it would take for the settlers to become self-sufficient.[17]

In North America, a group to found the colony of Liberia was established. The American Colonization Society was established in 1817 to send slaves to Africa which many people believed was their true home. But it caused controversy as it assumed blacks were incapable of receiving fair treatment in the so-called Land of the Free. Frederick Douglass believed black people should stay and fight for a better, fairer society for all, rather than accept being treated as a problem to be disposed of. African settlements were described as a "pernicious alternative" to abolition.[18] The British colony of Sierra Leone was claimed by its supporters as a precursor to abolition. Its first settlers arrived in 1822, and it is now the oldest black republic in Africa.

Gist had allowed the Virginia Assembly to make alternative arrangements, so they could have chosen this option. Gist made no mention of this in his will: it was added to the act which proved his will in Virginia, so has often been attributed to him. When Rev. Abdy visited Gist's settlements, he met a man who had returned from Liberia where he described a few settlers succeeding as merchants. But the main goal of freedmen becoming farmers had been a dismal failure. Wickham seems never to have considered this as a viable option, believing the climate and soil were unsuitable, which seems bizarre as others saw such resettlements as sending the freed slaves home. Perhaps he had doubts about the young colony; he may have worried about the cost as funds remained uncertain, or he may have doubted the freedmen's ability to survive without Europeans to support them.

The Virginia Court of Chancery delayed the final settlement of Gist's will until all the challenges had been resolved. In the meantime, there had been a very real danger that the estate might prove inadequate to pay the claims and even that some slaves might have been sold to satisfy the demands of the various claimants. The freedmen later complained that they had not been told of their manumission, but this was probably due to the prolonged uncertainty, though paternalism by the trustees was probably also a factor.

By 1828 Wickham was at last in control of what was left of the finances; about half of Gist's legacy had been paid out to settle the Anderson case, and Gist had never expected to incur the massive costs of moving so many people. Tales of Gist's huge estate seem to have created high expectations in his former slaves. Whatever happened to them, they were bound to be disappointed. Land in Free States had risen in price, while the slaves had increased in numbers, and they still had to be fed and cared for whilst they waited. They had been expected to continue working the land and helping to fund their manumission, but tobacco production ceased by 1819,[19] in expectation of their mass removal. It is not known how they spent their time: presumably working as some form of hired labour. During the War of 1812, trade was depressed, so they may have supported themselves on the remaining Gist lands. By 1824 only eleven thousand dollars was sent to the Quaker agents in Ohio.[20]

Yet it was not until February 14 1851 that the General Assembly of Ohio passed and act to allow the Court of Common Pleas of Highland Country to acquire jurisdiction over the funds which had been passed to the trustees under the Court of Chancery in Richmond Virginia. Gist's will was placed on the record there.[21] But this action is confusing, as the Highland County settlements were the smallest and most recent. It would have made more sense to pass responsibility to the Brown County courts. The Quaker agents as trustees were given the remaining funds and they were to present their accounts and vouchers to the court, so if they were cheating the freedmen, as was so often claimed, this court should have taken action. But the General Assembly was in Columbus, so a long way for the freedmen to travel for justice.

Gist's will claimed he wished his former slaves to be treated kindly. Wickham went to great efforts on his behalf, purchasing clothes and tools to help them establish themselves in their new lands. An often cited item was leather for shoes, which raises questions as to whether they had ever needed them in Virginia. Part of the hardship of the long trek to their new home may have involved getting used to wearing shoes for the first time on the hard roads.

Many authors complained of Wickham's performance, that he was overly protective, especially in his refusal to provide titles to the land. He believed this would encourage the freedmen to support each other and to protect the community. But to his credit, he stayed with the case through several decades, recording every action, every penny spent, in accordance with the conservative practices of the Court of Chancery. It is hard to justify any complaints against him for his time and effort. He claimed to know of several manumissions which had failed as slaves used their freedom to move elsewhere and their legacies were lost. Hence his insistence that the Gist communities remain united.

Gist showed insight in insisting on his freedmen being educated and given religious instruction. This should have provided them with tools to survive, a strong moral framework for their lives and access to language with which to engage with the wider society. He specified they be instructed according to the practices of the Protestant Church of England, so like Bristol's greatest benefactor Edward

Colston, it seems Gist was no supporter of Nonconformism. In England, members of the Anglican Church tended to be the establishment, whereas the various Nonconformists tended to be lower class and poorly or self-educated. Despite this, it seems Gist himself was not a churchgoer. He lived much of his life in London, but chose not to be buried there, so he seems not to have favoured a local parish church. None of his benefactions beyond the manumission were to religious groups or charities. Like many of his age, he seems to have viewed religion as a means of social advancement and support for the poor. The wealthy had better ways to spend their time.

Like white women, and children, the freedmen had no legal status, so had to be represented in court by a white man. William Fanning Wickham did his duty, but he was no radical, and probably didn't believe in what he was doing, as he continued to be a supporter of the institution of slavery. The freedmen often claimed he provided them with little support, and refused to reply to their letters requesting help, seeming unconcerned with by their plight. But after the long battle in chancery with the Anderson family and others, he was probably exhausted. He managed the affair until the last of the elderly freedmen in Virginia died, then he handed over the remaining funds to the estate trustees in Ohio. It is hard to see what more he could have done.

The lack of access to titles was a huge and ongoing issue as there were numerous cases where freedmen or their descendants sold their allocated plots to white people who were able to obtain titles and re-sell them. In the long term, the lack of ownership led to lack of investment, so —unlike the Quakers — they could not build up stable communities, with close networks based on mutual help and support. The limitations on their land as their families continued to grow led to numerous boundary disputes arising. An author also noted the "fishbowl factor" in which the communities were held up as examples for their race, so their every action would always be heavily weighted with significance and meaning.[22] In the 1820s only a few thousand black people lived in Ohio, so Gist's freedmen may have been the largest group there.[23] A less famous group was established by William Dunlop from Kentucky; he settled them about three miles north of Ripley in 1796, so they were close to the camp near Georgetown. Abdy's visit to the camps showed some of the freedmen were intelligent, morally sound and more than capable of hard work. They were also well aware that they would always struggle within a system that was stacked against them. Placing them in a neighbourhood of Quakers may have helped them, but when threatened with violence, they would have been left to their own devices.

In 1850 a group of Quakers condemned the freedmen's tendency towards vice and idleness which they claimed prevented their community flourishing, but they were measuring them by their own high standards, which was grossly unfair. The poor soil they were granted was often complained of, but it is unlikely that any whites wanted it, so it may have protected them from the worst racist abuses. They may have been condemned for not thriving, but to their credit, they did not resort to crime and immorality as was often predicted. At the very least, these settlements — though all but one have failed — have generated families that still gather in growing numbers to commemorate the legacy of an enigmatic Englishman.

Some commentators have noted the surnames of the freedmen and their descendants. Slaves had no surnames. They had no need for them as they belonged to their master and were mostly illiterate. When surnames evolved in Europe, they tended to describe a person, such as tall, or the name of their home, or their profession. There were also sons named after their fathers so men named William Williams can be found in historic records, sometimes in several generations, to the great annoyance of researchers. The list of Gist's slaves from 1787 includes Bristol and London; others had common names of the time such as Lucy, Abraham, Tom and Rachel. But there were also some oddities such as Suck, Lime and Myall. In the decades that followed the manumission, the surname Toler continued, probably the descendants of Gist's manager. But

Gist as a surname has died out. It has been suggested that the freedmen and their descendants felt let down by Gist, so changed their names, which is possible. But it is also possible that the name died out under natural circumstances, just as it did with the heirs of their benefactor back in England. But descendants of the Gist freedmen have his name, so perhaps it continued in the group that moved to New York or drifted away during the drawn-out removals.

9

CHOOSING THE LAND

When Gist wrote his will he hoped his former slaves would be allowed to stay together in Virginia. But the Virginian Assembly refused this, so Wickham was forced to find and purchase land and arrange for their emigration, which became a huge, expensive exercise.

Ohio was the closest Free State to Virginia, but the best land was in the south, along the Ohio River, so it was both expensive and scarce. It was also seen as dangerously close to Kentucky which would put the freedmen at risk of slave catchers who often attacked or stole people of colour irrespective of their legal status. Quakers, who supported abolition, had also settled in the state, so it was hoped they would support the settlers.

But Wickham seems to have been poorly informed as to the value of land as he intended to purchase three to five thousand acres of good soil, with healthy air.[1] If this was obtainable, it would have been prohibitively expensive. In later years, the region chosen for the settlement was described as "these wild lands were the only place where the Virginian or Southern masters could take their slaves and free them".[2] Wickham stated his intention to visit the area to purchase land in 1817, but for unknown reasons, failed to do so.[3]

Had he made this journey, he could probably have averted some of the subsequent problems.

When Ohio's constitution was being written, issues of race were sidelined by establishing white people as the legal norm. But two years later, only freedmen with a certificate of freedom could remain. By 1807 ex-slaves were also required to provide a five hundred dollar bond, so yet again it seems there were fears that they would not pay their own way. The early years of settlement in Ohio saw tobacco growing encouraged; this may have been part of the attraction for Gist's trustees, as the freedmen knew how to grow it, so it could provide them with a cash crop.

Wickham chose land in Brown County, on the northern bank of the wide Ohio River, which separated it from the Slave State of Kentucky. Ohio entered the States in 1802, and Brown Country was formed in 1803, from parts of Clermont and Adams Counties. It was part of the Revolutionary Lands, granted to southern veterans who fought in the War of Independence. But the area was still unsurveyed, so was uncleared. Before the freedmen could support themselves, a lot of hard work was required. A contemporary source claimed: "these flatlands were covered with water more than half of the year and were called slashes".[4] Even without local knowledge, the fact that the region was still unclaimed decades after the war ended should have raised questions with Wickham about its quality.

But this may have been seen as resembling Virginia, as a map of Hanover County shows a settlement called *Slash Church* to the southwest of Hanover Court House. Unlike Hanover Town, it survives. The term *slash* refers to ravines which form in soil after heavy rain. Rev. Patrick Henry preached there. The town of Ashland, which became a railroad resort in the early nineteenth century, was originally named *Slash Cottage*.[5]

§

General Richard Clough Anderson (1750–1826) was Principal Surveyor to the Military Lands. He was born in Hanover County, the son of Robert and Elizabeth (Clough) Anderson, making him first cousin to William Anderson, Gist's son-in-law, yet another reminder of how small their world was. It seems he could — and should — have been consulted on the quality of the soil before it was purchased.

The town of Ripley was a major port on the river, and an important crossing point for slaves fleeing the South. The land was claimed by Col. Poage of Virginia who was alleged to be opposed to slavery, in 1804, and renamed after Brigadier General Ripley following his heroism in the War of 1812,[6] so the town was very new when the freedmen passed through to their new homes. On Main Street is the Liberty Monument which commemorates many local abolitionists and members of the Underground Railroad who helped refugees on their way north. The Presbyterian minister John Rankin famously kept a light burning at his house above the town to guide fleeing slaves to freedom. John P. Parker, a slave who had purchased his own freedom as a teenager went further, bravely crossing the river to guide runaway slaves to freedom.

When the English traveller Rev. Abdy visited the region in 1833 he had expected local people to be supportive of the Gist settlement, but country people tend to visit towns for work and to sell farm produce. Ripley was a busy port, so people's knowledge of and connection with its hinterland was limited. It was a major stopping place on the Underground Railroad, but this involved providing short term shelter and aid to fleeing slaves. This was dangerous work, and they were not involved in their settlement or long-term welfare.

The first of the Gist settlements was five miles north of George-town, to the north of Ripley and the river. It became the seat of local government in 1821; it was described as well sited, with good views of surrounding farmland;[7] and in 1819 land there was priced at five dollars per acre. This description is at odds with the nearby swamplands so may have led to confusion in the Gist trustees. Most of the locals were white settlers were from the Slave States of

Virginia and Kentucky, including the family of Ulysses Grant.[8] Other settlers came from the north, especially Quakers. From 1787 slavery was banned north of the Ohio River.[9] Some may have chosen a Free State out of sympathy with slaves and even supported abolition, but were unlikely to want hundreds of freedmen as neighbours. Slavery kept down the wages of working white people, so opposition to it may not have involved any commitment to human rights or abolition per se. Similar conflicts were the basis of the nineteenth century White Australia policy, which was passed to stop the practice of "blackbirding", i.e. the kidnapping of Polynesians to work on the sugar plantations of Queensland which threatened the work of white labourers. Thus the act was to stop slavery and protect local wages but as times changed, it became a means of excluding migration by non-whites

Joshua Woodrow was paid by Wickham to survey the land for settlement and to construct log houses for the arrival of the first of the freedmen in 1819. In 1815 Cadwallader Wallace of Chillicothe had surveyed two tracts of land of one thousand and one thousand two hundred acres beside the White Oak and Straight Creeks. He was the government inspector of the Land Office at Chillicothe in Ross County.[10] He obtained three thousand acres of "flat, wet lands"[11] in six townships including Scott and Clark where the Gist freedmen were settled. He and Woodrow were responsible for taxes on seven hundred and sixty acres in Adams County from 1820–25, suggesting they were speculating in land, so Wilson's involvement as trustee was far from altruistic.[12] Had this been a speculation, or had he previously been commissioned to do this but the sale fell through? He offered to sell the land for four thousand four hundred dollars (i.e. two dollars per acre), and the deed was signed on 17 November 1818.[13]

This was a fraction of the value of land in Georgetown, but this was open, uncleared land, so this would be normal. But it is a lot for land that was known locally as being worthless. Historian P.K. Wright makes the extraordinary claim that Wickham agreed to exchange this waste for farmland[14] — apparently from Gist's estate. How could uncleared swamp be valued at the same rate as quality farmland in Virginia? Or is this evidence that land in Hanover County had fallen in value? Wright also notes conflicts in the acreage recorded in maps submitted to the Brown County Recorder's Office.[15] Wickham seems to have made a poor bargain from the outset.

Wright further claims that in 1826, Wallace surveyed another area of Brown County for a war veteran, but then claimed it as his own. He lost the court case and was forced to pay damages, so he seems to have been a poor choice as surveyor. When the Gist settlers arrived, and the land was shown to be worth far less than had been paid for it, why did Gist's executors or agents not take action against Wallace? If the settlement was sold as farmland, why did they not demand he pay for it to be cleared and improved so the freedmen would have a chance of survival —if not of success — in their new homes? Complaints were later made that the agents employed to support the freedmen lived too far away to be able to fulfil this role. They must have known that the land was worthless. So it seems the choice of agents was also questionable. With such a disastrous start, the settlements were doomed from the outset.

In 1819 the first move involved one hundred and nineteen of Gist's former slaves from Amherst and Goochland counties were taken to the Upper Settlement of one thousand acres in Eagle Township, west of the town of Fincastle in Brown County. Another source claims one thousand four hundred and seventeen acres were surveyed, of which one thousand one hundred and ninety-seven were divided in 1819 into thirty-two lots between one hundred and fifty freedmen.[16] These people were already struggling when the lower settlement of one thousand two hundred acres in Scott Township, north of Georgetown, was founded with fifty-eight people from Hanover County in 1821.[17] The other source claims one thousand one hundred and twenty-one acres were divided into thirty-one lots between one hundred and thirteen freedmen in July 1819.[18] It is hard to make sense of all these inconsistencies in the records, but this helps explain how the freedmen's descendants had so much trouble establishing what they were owed and who owned what land.

Details of the trek from Virginia to Ohio are hard to find; their journey was long before proper roads were built. As the crow flies, it is hundreds of miles, but mention was made of them travelling along the Ohio River. Niles' Weekly Register published in Baltimore on 30 June 1821 described this second group of freedmen going to the settlement near Georgetown, Ohio. It described fifty-eight freed slaves passing through Washington, Pennsylvania. This seems to be a huge detour to the north, but they were a few miles from the Ohio River, so by then the worst of their journey seems to have been over. The account claimed they had three wagons to carry their goods and their behaviour was described as "quite orderly", and they were apparently grateful for their master's philanthropy towards them.[19] This article also shines some light on the high costs of moving the freedmen. If it took three wagons to move fifty-eight, the overall costs must have been huge.

The slaves who Gist freed were apparently illiterate, so have left no records of their lives or early struggles, but fortunately a traveller from England wrote of his visits to several of the settlements. Edward Strutt Abdy (1791–1846) of Albyns, in Essex was a graduate of Jesus College, Cambridge who studied law but never practised it due to poor health. He seems to have had no employment, so must have inherited enough to live and travel. He was a member of the Society for the Improvement of Prison Discipline and Reformation of Juvenile Offenders whose visit to the United States resulted in the publication of *A Journal of a Residence and Tour in the United States of North America From April 1833 to October 1834*, which was published the following year and which described his visits to several of the Gist settlements. When he died in Bath, probably seeking a cure in 1846 he left several bequests including five hundred pounds to Maria Weston Chapman of Boston for her work on abolishing American slavery, so she probably inspired his visit.

He visited Rev. Rankin at his house above Ripley, where he kept a light burning to guide slaves fleeing along the Underground Railroad. The Gist settlements were still called camps, so had not thrived in the decade since they were established. When Abdy reached the first camp, north of Georgetown, he met a family who claimed they had never been told in Virginia that they had been freed, and continued in ignorance when they were transported. They believed the land in Virginia where they worked had been left to them, so they were confused when they were forced to leave. This explains their resistance to their relocation from the outset. Clarification had been provided by an old man, a former servant of Gist who promised to help them, but after he left, they believed he was poisoned. What a shame they didn't recall his name for this to be investigated. Gist's will named a single servant, Thomas Gibbons, so it may have been him.

When the slaves realised they were free, they refused to work any more so were beaten, a practice they had never before known. They spoke of Gist's kindness as a master, who continued to send them good blankets and clothes after he left. They also praised his daughters.

By the time of Abdy's visit in 1833, the camps were about fifteen years old, but, not surprisingly, had struggled from the outset. He described the land as being the most unsuitable in the worst part of the Union, "as they can neither live upon the produce of their allotments, nor obtain work without being liable to be defrauded by men who shelter their iniquity under the cloak of the law".[20] Thus, their problems were social as well as geographical. He praised neighbouring Quakers who had arrived with wagons and boats full of food, tools and clothing, i.e. items that should have come from Gist's bequest, without which they would have starved in the woods. But this had been an emergency measure for the first winter; they could not have been expected to repeat it.

This highlights another problem for the relocation: long-distance travel with wagons was best done in spring/summer when the roads were passable, and the travellers were not at risk of storms, so could sleep in the open air. But in order to plant crops, they needed to arrive at the end of winter, so the resettlements were doomed by this conundrum which seems not to have been considered by Wickham.

Abdy's hosts at the camp near Georgetown described the horrors of their long journey from Virginia, of the undrained and uncleared land they were given, and the lack of tools to work it. Families were granted plots in proportion to the size of their family group, but their numbers continued to increase, and they were unable to obtain more land. Some white neighbours were hostile, so work was scarce and they were poorly paid and exploited. A few found work on the river or moved to Cincinnati. They were often raided at night, at risk from slave traders and even expected to accommodate travellers without payment. Abdy was told of a local storekeeper who had exploited them and who fled with his spoils to Illinois.

They claimed Wickham had promised to visit, which seems unlikely given he was a busy man hundreds of miles away. They complained of having to pay local taxes and repair roads, just as their white neighbours did, but receiving no protection from the law in return. A law was later passed exempting non-whites from paying school taxes as they were excluded from the education system. The freedmen spoke of being harassed and threatened by whites, mostly from the nearby towns. In Georgetown, three miles south of the first camp, a colonization society[21] was formed to promote the removal of slaves to Liberia, so there was marked hostility to their presence. This group may have been inspired by the failure of the settlements, leading locals to believe the freedmen were incapable of maintaining themselves.

Abdy also spoke to the agent Woodrow, who was the subject of many complaints. He suggested the freedmen were fond of whiskey, which the Englishman thought was unlikely. When he arrived at their settlement he was in considerable distress, the result of long-term ill health. He was welcomed into their home, and invited to stay the night. Their concern for him should have extended to offering him whiskey as medicine if they had any. They complained of having no one to support them, despite the agents being expected to fulfil this role. He predicted that without support, the lower camp would soon be abandoned.

The Englishman met several local white people who confirmed

the abuses, but justified them on the grounds that the freedmen had no right to be there and should be sent back to Africa. They claimed it would be easy to evict them as they had not been granted titles to their land. Abdy was horrified by these opinions, claiming this would bankrupt the country by the removal of its hardest workers. Granting land to freedmen may also have been resented by local settlers who had had to pay for their own land, making the freedmen seem lazy. Though of course, most of the slaves had paid for the land by their lifelong servitude.

Abdy also spoke to a family who had returned from Africa, having been sent there by the charity Brown Company Colonization Society. They claimed a third of the settlers died within a year, that starvation, abuse and embezzlement were rife and the few who thrived did so as merchants rather than farmers. Abdy left this camp believing that the residents' lives would improve if schools were established, with white people in charge to support and protect them. But even so, this still left the freedmen with no legal redress, so they would continue to be vulnerable. There were also problems of distance: the agents had been appointed by the Manumission Society of Philadelphia through the Virginian courts, so were a long way away. Of the three agents, only Enoch Lewis lived near the settlement.

A decade after the two camps in Brown County were established, the Court of Chancery in Richmond, Virginia passed an order to transport the rest of Gist's freedmen to Ohio. But it seems Wickham had still not learned from the failures of the earlier resettlements as he bought five hundred and forty acres of land in Sandusky, Ohio. But it was even worse than the previous camps, full of standing water for most of the year which bred mosquitoes and illnesses, so they all retuned to Virginia. Another source claimed white settlers had threatened to kill them, and even to set local Indians onto them.[22]

Trotti claimed this was a small tract near Sandusky in North

Ohio which was abandoned by fifty settlers soon after they arrived. Another source claims this was two hundred and thirty negroes were moved to six hundred and forty acres, but this land was abandoned due to mosquitoes and malaria.[23] They were probably from Hanover County, and included those who had returned or evaded previous removals. They apparently returned to Virginia in the early 1820s, which challenges claims that whites had given them an ultimatum to depart by a certain date. It seems more likely that they had been content in Virginia and failed to see whey they should leave. This view is further strengthened by Wickham's claim that a family remained there up to 1831 when the land was sold.

Finally, Wickham bought one hundred acres of allegedly good farmland in Highland County for eight hundred dollars in 1832. It was about eighteen miles north-west of the Eagle Settlement. He seems to have learnt at last from his mistakes Friendly neighbouring Quakers were paid to improve the land and sow crops to prevent the new settlers starving in their first year.[24] But they were soon neglected by their agents and there was probably an increase in their numbers, so a further purchase of land was made in 1835, of one hundred and seven acres in Fairford (now Penn) Township for five hundred dollars.[25]

This last group seems to have been made up of seventy who had remained behind. Abdy claimed they were hiding as they did not wish to leave. They were rounded up in 1829; they had maintained themselves in the interim by farming land they had lived on, as it was untenanted at the time. At times, the resettlement of the freedmen seems to have been akin to herding cats, which shows how independent they were. The final removal seems to have included several people who were not part of the original group and it is unclear what happened to the final family at the abandoned settlement of Sardinia in Highland County when the rest returned to Virginia. This move became complicated as the freedmen must have known of the many problems in the earlier settlements. Some refused to leave; others chose, and were paid, to go to New York instead. Accounts note how several were transported in handcuffs. Wickham held on to the remaining funds to support the group of five elderly and infirm who were incapable of making the long trek. When the last of these died in 1847, the trust fund in Virginia was closed and the money sent to the agents in Ohio. Wickham's legal career ended the same year and he became a planter. Perhaps the marathon of managing Gist's estate had been the final straw.

One of the freedmen at the new settlement raised some important questions with Abdy. Since the agents had never seen a copy of Gist's will, how could they implement it, or defend the lack of funds for the freedmen? Abdy promised to provide them with a copy of Gist's will when he returned to England and included a copy in the appendix of his journal when it was published. He also noted the many problems the freedmen faced in obtaining justice, from the amount of time that had passed, the claims of relatives, tricks played by agents, the actions of the Virginia courts, the physical distance between the Britain and North America, the lack of education of the freedmen and their inability to pursue justice in the courts.

From this distance in time, it may be hard to make sense of the repeated agricultural failures of the freedmen when nearby farmers were far more successful. But the first settlers could choose the best land, and the Quakers were an extraordinarily successful group, educated, knowledgeable and bound together by their shared beliefs, business and family ties. Migrants traditionally moved to areas similar to their origins,[26] so the Quakers probably understood the local soil.

The move from Virginia to Ohio was a huge change for the freedmen, from the rich alluvial soil of the Tidewater. Yet Wickham may have believed the waterlogged soil was similar to that of Virginia, so would be suitable for farming. It is unclear if they were planting the same crops that they were used to or if they had to adapt to local situations. Moving even a short distance may have exposed them to new organisms, new illnesses which may have impaired their health enough to reduce their capacity to work. They had always been supervised, which raises questions as to whether they were prepared for their new, independent lives. They had little use for initiative whilst enslaved, yet the opposition by some to their removal shows they were aware of alternatives, were engaged with and informed of the wider world. Some authors condemn the level of control and paternalism shown by the various trustees and agents, but this was a cyclical system. If slaves were not encouraged to show initiative, they did not demonstrate it, which further entrenched negative attitudes towards them. And again, they had no legal status, so — like white women — could not give evidence in court, nor take actions against others.

Abdy visited the colony in Highland County a year after it was founded, but he found conditions were already similar to those at the Lower Camps. They were closer to the agents, so expected more help but they were also struggling with poor land and their lack of ownership of it. They complained of the trustee and storekeeper Enoch who refused to supply them with raw materials or money to buy what they needed, forcing them to choose items from his store. When they needed clothing, they were required to buy items made by his daughter, rather than make their own, so he was free to exploit them.[27] The control vested in the trustees was intended to prevent the freedmen from being exploited by unscrupulous businesses, but it allowed them to exploit the community with impunity.

The historical marker at the final settlement in Fairfield lists the names of the thirty-one original plots. They suggest that at last Gist's will was being implemented, as a plot each was allocated to the cemetery and the board of education, so a church and school were to be built. Of the remainder, fourteen were owned by women, with Hester Day having two. This suggests the community had lost a lot of the men, was highly matriarchal, or that the men were forced to work away, so the women were left to run the settlement in their absence.

In the fourth codicil of Gist's will, he made allowances in case his slaves could not be freed. He noted "the great increase of my negroes, there being upwards of one hundred under the age of ten years of age,", suggesting that as they grew up there would not be enough land to employ them, so instructed his executors to sell three thousand 5% stocks to buy "the most convenient lands adjoining any other lands as it can be bought", so he expected the population of his slaves to increase significantly in a short space of time. This became a problem which was ignored by many accounts and which could not have been allowed for by his legacy, especially after it had been so depleted by the legal challenges by the Anderson heirs.

When Abdy visited Highland County, he met Peter Vise who complained his family had only been provided with three hoes to work the land, and that his allocation of eighty acres was insufficient to feed his family of sixteen. Several of his sons had left to find work elsewhere, especially in Cincinnati. Whilst his farm was highly productive, there was no way Gist's legacy could provide for the exponential growth of this and other families.

But it was also a problem with white families and which drove many young people to abandon their land, to learn trades, move to cities, and to the expansion of European settlement in North America. The land the freedmen were issued with may have been sufficient when they arrived, but within a generation, their large families had overstretched their limited resources. It also shows how effective had been the many checks and balances on human communities in Europe before the Reformation, where populations were reasonably stable. Suggestions have been made that infanticide was widely practised, but lack of housing for newlyweds, backed up with shame about intimacy outside wedlock seems to have been major factors in Europe. With the best of intentions, Gist could not have made allowances for the constant increase in the number of his freedmen.

This also raises questions as to the treatment of Gist's slaves. Accounts survive from November 1783, i.e. almost two decades after Gist returned to England, and they show a heavy bias towards the very young. Two men are listed as sixty, a few are fifty and a few more of forty, which may be normal for the age, but about half were under ten. This may mean that the slaves liked each other, or it could have been that they were encouraged to breed, especially during the war when supplies of slaves from Africa and the West Indies had been expensive or impossible to obtain.

By 1835 the settlements were cited by their opponents as examples of the folly of emancipation, as they had become "wretched and unproductive",[28] so fed into the racist stereotypes of lazy slaves. But the author of the article recalled meeting the younger members of the original community, who had by then become the elders. He described them as being victims of a situation which would have shocked the government and charities.[29] He claimed that accusations of them being ignorant were perhaps true, as they had been deprived of the education which Gist had planned for them, but he denied they were depraved, though their lives would have forced many to become so. He also expressed surprise that such conditions could exist so close to the Underground Railroad, where they could have expected more help.

Research is beginning to clarify the role the Gist settlements played in the Underground Railroad. The settlements were all located on the main line of flight of slaves fleeing northwards, which suggests the freedmen offered shelter and support, but this same positioning must also have attracted the attention of slave catchers and put them at risk of attack from racist neighbours.

The last of the Gist trustees was William D. Huggins who died in 1885; he was involved in the Railroad. Runaway slaves tended to cross the Ohio River, and from Ripley headed north to Scot Township and then to Sardinia. Eagle Township was home to John Hudson, a major conductor on the Railroad, showing the Highland Country settlements were also significant. Some residents of the various Gist settlements seem to have been highly mobile, so could have spread information which helped warn of impending dangers, as did slaves who had fled from Kentucky who sometimes worked in Ohio.

But the settlements took huge risks by aiding the runaway slaves. In 1839 a resident of Eagle Settlement, Sally Hudson was murdered.[30] More incidents probably occurred but due to the under-reporting of people of colour, have left few traces. Their involvement may have been a conscious decision, or they may have been drawn into the process by their isolation and geography. When Abdy arrived at a farm after dark, he had to convince the inhabitants that he meant them no harm, and was eventually treated with much kindness and hospitality, even though they had little to feed themselves.

10

FOLLOW THE MONEY

The sheer size of Gist's will shows he put a lot of time and thought into it, yet he still left a number of financial matters in Virginia which sowed the seeds for problems that echo down to the present time.

The story of the Gist freedmen is littered with claims of what went wrong, and where the Englishman's vast wealth ended up. Many people in the USA — from various descendants of the freedmen to journalists and lawyers — have invested enormous amounts of time and effort in trying to trace the story, but with limited success. Claims have been made of financial mismanagement by trustees, of theft by heirs on both sides of the Atlantic, even that the British government stole millions of pounds from the estate. Given how much time has passed, no simple answer is possible. Many records are incomplete or contradictory. Much of the research has been driven by the noble search for justice, an attempt to establish some form of legacy for the descendants of Gist's slaves. But in order to establish where the money went, it is necessary to find out how it was acquired.

The paper trail is hampered by the loss of many original documents in a fire which destroyed much of the city of Richmond and its records in 1885. No personal papers of Gist and others have survived. The story is littered with gaps and occasional errors, such as the often repeated claim that Gist had imported the first thoroughbred racehorse into North America in 1730, which is an impressive achievement, made even more so by the fact that Gist was a young child in Britain at the time.

Another major issue is the quality of the legal system at the time. The Virginia Company's main aim in settling the area was to make money. In 1612 the first tobacco crop was planted and with the first House of Burgesses established at Jamestown, the region was soon self governing. But the seventeenth century in England was one of the most unstable periods in British history and educational standards were low, so standards of governance were likewise.

Britain's much maligned class system meant that those at the top of society were generally well educated, so understood the practices of government and law. In Shakespeare's history plays, kings were surrounded by older, wiser advisors, some of whom were clerics, so understood how the world operated though their knowledge of the classics, the Bible, and a lifetime of public service. There are even instances when the audience is consulted, reflecting how small was the world and how common was the need for outside advice.

Society was bound together by mutually supporting classes. Large landowners received rents from tenants, and in return supported them financially during crises such as famines, and helped rebuild communities after floods or fire, as well as being responsible for maintaining local charities. Such practices held communities together, though in the eighteenth century, with the rise of absentee landlords, abuse and exploitation became widespread. If a local justice was unfair in his judgements, locals sometimes retaliated by rioting or vandalising his property, the risks of which generally held the wealthy to account.

But in the colonies, legal disputes were often resolved on the basis of personal loyalties rather than the rule of law. Juries supported their neighbouring smallholders while justices supported their wealthy friends and relatives. People were said to be quarrelsome due to the immense strains they were under, living in such unstable times. Many resorted to the courts to resolve disputes, so the system became clogged up with cases, and witnesses were often fined for non-attendance, which led to cases collapsing, and wasting even more court time. Apparently one of the most famous cases was brought by Samuel Gist against Samuel and Caroline Riddick, who were alleged to have ridiculed his efforts in the French and Indian War.[1]

༅

Gist was described as a 'shop boy' to John Smith, having been trained as a scrivener and in the maintenance of accounts, though it is unclear whether part of this was with the Lyde business before he was sent abroad to help in Smith's shop. The term 'shop' implies a small, local affair, but it was a complex business that provided most of the items locals were unable to grow or make for themselves, so included everything from bricks and beer to rifles and ribbons. Smith was also an agent for English tobacco merchants which is how he arranged to obtain young Gist as his apprentice, as his sons were too young to help him. Hanover Town was a major port, the reason for its existence, providing a vital link between Virginian planters and Britain, especially Bristol and London.

Several of Gist's surviving letters from England to his stepson John Smith jun. show they had to understand shipping and negotiate with various merchants for imports and exports, for space on ships, and to predict demand for goods. The local currency from the earliest times was tobacco, which varied from season to season, making it difficult to adhere to budgets, so shopkeepers had to deal with many variables. They also had to understand the complexities of the tobacco trade, which was crucial to the region. Paper money was seldom used and rarely trusted.

Few planters arrived with sufficient capital to buy land, plant it then survive till they received the money for their first crop, so had to survive on credit for a year, but if anything went wrong, debts could easily mount up. The local economy was based largely on credit and barter due to problems with poor quality coinage, and by the middle of the century, coin balances were increasingly common to confirm the content of heavy gold and silver. A single storm could devastate the local economy; neglect in pest control could wipe out a crop, and the loss of a ship could destroy a planter's business. Many growers shared the risk by having multiple investors, a practice which gave rise to the insurance industry in which Gist seems to have become so successful in London. But it also meant that when people died, they often owned part shares in other businesses which in turn could be passed on, so wills could be incredibly complicated and give rise to multiple challenges and disputes, further overwhelming the court system. Overseas payments were mostly via a letter of credit which was presented to the client's bank. But if the client's credit was poor at the time, this could be refused, and the seller plunged into debt.

Gist seems to have been an astute student of business, arriving as a penniless orphan in the colony and grew up to become a business partner of some of its most affluent planters such as Washington and Bacon. When John Smith jun. died in 1754 his estate was passed to his two sons, but as they were underage, Gist was appointed their guardian. Gist ran the Smith business on their behalf until they came of age when their father's estate was divided between them, with John acquiring the shop in Hanover Town and Joseph the plantation of Gould's Hill. The Hanover Rent Roll for 1763 provides an insight into the nature of the business, with John Smith jun. being listed as owning two hundred acres, probably to feed himself and provide a tobacco crop, and his brother Joseph owning eight hundred and eighty acres of Gould's Hill.[2] The dates of birth and death of both sons are unclear, but John should have been the eldest as he was named after his father. Yet in several documents his brother was named as his guardian, which adds confusion to this.

But the amount of money and land passed on to the Smith sons was further complicated by the complex system of family inheritance. John Massie of Goochland County died in 1743 without issue. His plantations were said to be some of the oldest in the region which sounds impressive, but this may mean that the soil had become exhausted, so was of little value. His will demonstrates the complexities of inheritance, including legacies to pay off debts, to acknowledge loyalty and friendship, and as acts of charity for poor relatives and servants.

He left ten pounds to each of his brothers on condition it was not used to pay off debts. Money was left to his nieces and nephews but it was to be paid out of the produce of the estate, not from land sales. This shows his determination to keep his estate intact, to ensure its continued viability. But this meant that if the crops failed or if something happened to his slaves, they would receive nothing.

John Smith's wife was variously referred to as Mary or Sarah, Massie or Smith, which has caused confusion in many of the records. Samuel and his wife Mary Smith as executors swore in 1758 that profits from the Massie estate had not been enough to pay all the debts and legacies in his will.[3] But in 1760 when the couple failed to provide the court with an account of the estates, they were ordered to pay the legacy to Massie's niece Anne Pinchbeck.[4] In another challenge, a niece died before she was old enough to inherit. Her family tried to claim the money, but were refused.

John Massie was uncle to Mary Smith, to whom he left some slaves for her lifetime. The bulk of the estate went to her husband, his nephew John Smith; land in England was mentioned but not named, and in Virginia, which amounted to over two hundred acres each in Henrico and Goochland Counties. The will is confusing as he refers to his executor John Smith as his "loving brother",[5] so it is unclear what their relationship was. They may have been of similar age, so grew up together.

But this makes the relationship between John and his wife unclear. How closely related were they? For Smith to be trusted with such an estate, he must have been a reliable and respected member of local society. The will was challenged by Massie's brother Peter on the basis of his being heir-at-law, so a direct blood relative, but this would only apply if a person died intestate. Massie's estate comprised the Middle Quarter, Old Quarter in Goochland County, and Dundee and Woodberry in Hanover County.[6] All these eventually became Gist's property

John Smith died in 1746 at the age of sixty, leaving his wife Mary and two young sons, John junior and Joseph. Gist married Mary two years later. She was a decade older than him but this was common practice. Due to the high incidence of women dying in childbirth, men often married several times, usually young, healthy spouses, to ensure the continuity of their name and wealth, so marriages between people of similar ages were not common. A choice of partner was often made on the basis of each being in good health, with an ability to work hard and be willing to compromise.

Only part of John Smith's will survives, in which he left his wife a third of his land and slaves for life, one fifth of his personal estate forever, and on her death, the slaves were to be divided between their sons, subject to any outstanding claims from the Massie estate.[7]

Gist became the legal guardians of John Smith's young sons, John jun. and Joseph, and also took charge of the estates of Smith and of Massie. He inherited houses with four hundred and forty acres of land in Hanover County and purchased a further one thousand nine hundred and sixty acres: the Old and Middle Quarter from his wife's relatives in Goochland and Amherst Counties. This helped him become one of the largest landowners and richest merchants in Hanover County. In 1777, six hundred acres made up of Woodberry and Bickerton plantations in Hanover Counties were bought by William Anderson on Gist's behalf, followed by Massies in 1782.[8] The same source added Amherst, noted as trust funds, but no details were provided of the acreage.[9] These estates were probably the first to be sold to fund the manumission, as slaves were moved from there.

§.

In the Virginia Historical Society archives are two accounts of Gist's slaves and the land they worked which date from November 1783.[10] They name The Old Quarter, Middle Quarter and Massie's Plantation in Goochland, and Woodberry and Dundee in Hanover County. The last of these was home to Gist's daughter Mary and her husband William Anderson. Gist had managed these estates during his stepsons' minorities, as well as running the store and all his other financial dealings; it seems he acquired them as a result of his stepsons' poor business skills which left them bankrupt at their deaths, which made him a very rich man and formed the basis of even greater wealth when he returned to England.

The Virginia Historical Society also holds a rent roll for Hanover County, showing the acreages of landowners, which mostly covers the year 1763, shortly before Gist departed. It was provided by Gist as part of his claim to the British government for compensation for the loss of his estates when they were confiscated by the Virginian House of Burgesses on the grounds that he was a loyalist, hence a traitor. Thus, it is a snapshot of landlords and estates at the time, providing a valuable insight into Gist's wealth and putting it into context with the wider population. It also shows that Gist had access to this record, and that he took it with him when he left.

There were a few large estates — remnants of the original grants — such as one of three thousand acres owned by Nelson Barkley, descended from the West Country aristocratic family. Nathaniel West Dandridge owned seven thousand two hundred and fifty-seven acres and William Fantleroy three thousand four hundred and thirty-three. But top of this tree was William Nelson Esq. with fourteen thousand eight hundred and fifty. At the lowest end of the scale were the likes of Elkanah Baughin, James Hall and William Howard with only fifty acres each, but they may not have subsistence farmers. They could have been tradesmen whose land supplemented their main incomes. Patrick Henry jun. owned three hundred and forty-three acres, and his father the Reverend of the same name had two plots totalling six hundred and thirty acres which he probably inherited. Washington's stepson Daniel Parkes Custis owned nine hundred and eleven acres. Gist had two plantations of two thousand four hundred and fife hundred and sixty. But the list helpfully noted he later purchased six hundred acres from John Bickerton and three hundred and fifty from George Cocke, giving him an impressive total of three thousand nine hundred and ten pounds, to make him one of the largest landowners in the county. As noted already, he also had land in other counties. His son-in-law William Anderson was from a large family; thirteen of them owned a total of four thousand nine hundred and sixty-five acres, with the largest being William's father with one thousand two hundred and forty-four.[11]

The above account was made when Gist's stepsons were adults, which puts their dates of birth pre 1742. John Smith jun. had two hundred acres, probably attached to or linked with the shop. Joseph owned eight hundred and eighty acres, which apparently belonged to Gould's Hill. This shows Gist by then had his own source of income, building up a property portfolio of land where he grew tobacco and traded on behalf of others. He later owned several ships, and was involved in slave trading.

But he and his wife claimed the Massie estate had been unprofitable, so it is unclear if those properties had contributed to his rising wealth. He probably invested wisely in other ventures which have left no easily found paper trail. Gist also acquired his wife's dowry, which should have been placed in safe hands on her marriage, but there is no record of what happened to it. This practice of spreading his risks, of not putting all his eggs in one basket seems to have provided him with a solid financial basis for his career.

Gist was active in the local community, serving on the Hanover County Court and as a parish officer for the church. With George Washington, he was one of twelve founders of the Dismal Swamp Company and the only one to make any money from this attempt to drain the region for farmland. He was also part of a committee authorised in 1750 to develop one hundred thousand acres on the New River, with four years to complete the surveys,[12] so he was respected and wealthy, and an innovator. He was the main witness for the Parson's Cause Case when Patrick Henry argued for the payment of wages to a local cleric. When Gist returned to England he imported the future president Washington's tobacco.

§&.

In 1752 Gist announced in the Virginia Gazette his intention to return to England, so his duty of care for his stepsons was ended. In the same year he became a burgess in Bristol, so he planned to settle in his home city at the age of about twenty-nine. But his plans fell through, possibly due to a problem in arranging guardianship of his stepsons. Instead, he became an agent for the Brown & Parks tobacconists while continuing to trade with his former patron Lyde.

Claiming poor health, Gist did return to England, in about 1765. Given he lived for several more decades, this seems unlikely, but as many people — including his step sons — died young, this cannot be dismissed. The region was low-lying, so was a fertile breeding ground for insects such as mosquitoes and the diseases they spread such as malaria. This suggests he had stayed long enough to discharge his responsibilities and that — like his patrons the Lydes — he had never called Virginia his home. He left his wife behind; some accounts claim he intended her to join him, but she died soon after in Maryland. Gist was joined by his daughters but his eldest — the still-underage Mary —eloped to Scotland with William Anderson in February 1768. He claimed in a letter:

> "I have not seen her & sincerely hope I never shall as she has almost killed me by this act of undutifullness".[13]

But the outbreak of the Revolutionary War in 1775 meant that Gist — as a loyalist and enemy — risked confiscation of all his lands. So in 1782 he arranged for an act to be passed in the Virginia General Assembly which vested all his properties in Mary in perpetuity. It seems his heart was mended by the need to save his bacon. Or perhaps, in view of his later manumission, he wanted to keep control of his estates to prevent abuse of his slaves. In Gist's will, he claimed this transfer of ownership was only temporary, but the act made it permanent.

In the Virginia Gazette of 1774 Anderson advertised the sale of several properties of the late John Smith jun., so he had become the executor for Gist's late stepsons. Smith's property comprised two hundred acres each in Hanover and Goochland Counties and the reversion of a tract of contiguous lands in the latter county then owned by Gist. All of these seem to have been from the Massie estate, and which soon became the property of Gist. But the advertisement noted that the latter property had a very curious condition, i.e. that the purchaser would acquire Gist's property when the old man died.[14] What was being advertised here? Was it one or both properties? If the owner sought to get two properties for the price of one, he was probably disappointed, as Gist continued to evade the Grim Reaper.

William and Mary Anderson left Virginia in September 1785.[15] Until then, they managed Gist's estates, followed his orders and sent him the profits. They also purchased several properties on his behalf, on condition that Gist repaid him, but he never did. This would not have mattered as they expected to become his main heirs. But Gist's longevity was equal to his business acumen.

&

Like many Britons, Gist viewed the War of Independence as a passing spat, a child struggling against the restrictions of its parents before seeing — or being forced to admit — the error of its ways. In his home town of Bristol, speculators built large breweries and other businesses which, with five brickworks, went spectacularly bankrupt after peace was declared, plunging the city into a massive financial depression. They had expected to return to pre-war conditions of trade and affluence, but the war taught the Americans the values of self-reliance. Skilled emigrants arrived, and slaves and freedmen with initiative became tradesmen. When peace came, the former colony had less need for imports from Europe. The victory over Britain was not just political; it was also financial and technical.

William Anderson's will of 1797 made his wife, Mary, and his father-in-law trustees for his nephew Francis and niece Mary, Anderson's orphaned relatives whom he and Mary had adopted after failing to produce children of their own. William called Gist his 'dear friend', rather than father-in-law, but was displeased at his refusal to pay for the Virginia land that had been purchased on his behalf, i.e. the Woodberry and Massie plantations. Disputes over these lands in Virginia continued till 1824.[16] Gist muddied the situation by claiming these were part of his lands vested in Mary by the 1782 act. William Anderson's relatives claimed he should be the owner, which Gist disputed.[17] But if it was William Anderson's then it should have descended to his widow. If Anderson's heirs had disputed his will, this should have been raised by them when he died, not during the settlement of Gist's estate.

The properties in Gist's will that had not been paid for were Woodberry in Hanover County, and Massies in Goochland. But when William Fanning Wickham began implementing the manumission of Gist's slaves, he sold part of the latter in 1805 for under six thousand dollars and the remainder was sold in 1819 for eleven thousand dollars.[18] William Anderson claimed he had bought the land, which led to his heirs claiming they should inherit the land plus decades of interest that had gone to Gist. This was disputed on the grounds that Anderson had never claimed to own the land, nor was he involved in its management. For a time there seemed a risk that the slaves might be drawn into the dispute and sold as chattels under Virginia law, as they were disposable via wills. To their credit, the Anderson heirs did not dispute the manumission, so it seems they shared William's support for the process. But by reducing the amount of land to pay for the manumission, they endangered the process. The Anderson family eventually won their case in 1825 and were awarded over eleven thousand dollars, about half of Gist's Virginian wealth.[19]

William Anderson wished the title to the land to be provided after Gist had paid his estate the original purchase price, twenty years' interest that he had gained from it, and the costs of improvements, taxes and obtaining the titles. This land was overseen by Gist's manager, so had no connection with Anderson. He left his wife all his rights to her father's former land, which had been vested in her by the 1782 act by the State of Virginia. Gist had rescued his land from the State of Virginia, only to lose it to his daughter.

Anderson bequeathed all his Virginia slaves to his mother for her lifetime, asking for them to be treated "humanely and kindly" and stated that they were to be freed on his death if laws at the time permitted. This was almost a decade before Gist wrote similar terms in his will, suggesting they were of a similar mindset.

᠗

Following the huge flight of slaves to the British army and Canada during the Revolutionary War, the Virginia Assembly made private emancipations easier, and about fifteen thousand were subsequently freed. This was probably to cope with the post-war manpower shortage which would have made it difficult or impossible to manage so many slaves. It was also a decade before Britain abolished the slave trade, the motives for which are still disputed. Declining soil fertility was probably a major factor, threatening the viability of crops such as tobacco and sugar. But France began planting sugar beet, reducing the value of West Indian imports, which was probably the most important reason. Advertisements for properties in the Tidewater region showing they were increasingly producing corn for export to Britain and the West Indies plantations rather than tobacco, seem to reflect this.

William Anderson's will created the first — and greatest — of the many problems that arose in the implementing of Gist's legacies, as the old man never paid for the land bought on his behalf, much of which adjoined the former estates of the Smiths and the Massies. This suggests Gist was failing to manage his business, yet after the War of Independence, Gist used the courts of Virginia to pursue debtors, some of whom owed him only a few pounds. He demanded payment from people who had lost everything when Cornwallis burned the town of Norfolk.

Gist didn't need the money, so why did he pursue his customers with such vengeance? This suggests Gist had a Midas-like obsession with money, or perhaps he failed to comprehend the damage done to the region and saw the failure to pay debts as a failure in trust, that the colonials were behaving in an ungentlemanly way. Or it may, as many authors suggest, this was more a hatred of colonials. He eventually retrieved about one thousand five hundred pounds, and his attorney John Wickham pursued compensation claims for losses during the war through federal courts.

When William and Mary Anderson returned to Virginia after their marriage, Gist wished them to live miserably, and it seems his wish came true. Anderson was sometimes referred to as a captain; one source[20] claims this means he was a militia officer to the Revolutionary Army and provided them with horses. But another source claims he was a ship's master;[21] if the latter is true, he seems to have abandoned the sea on his marriage.

By the time the couple returned to England, after managing Gist's estate and trading in tobacco, they owned Dundee Plantation. This included a brick house that had been built by John Smith in about 1768 of which only the foundations remain. It overlooked the Pamunkey River, a mile from Hanover Court House.[22] In the 1783 accounts by Gist's estate manager Benjamin Toler, it was home to forty-eight slaves. Many of Gist's properties seem to have belonged to the Smith and Massie families, which has led to allegations that he committed theft or fraud to obtain them, but it seems he purchased them after they left his adopted family's ownership.

There was a further dispute, initiated by Thomas Reade Rootes jun. in 1805, the year Gist wrote his will. It further threatened the manumission, and was complex due to the convoluted lines of family descent. When Gist's stepson John Smith jun. died unmarried and apparently intestate in about 1773 and Joseph followed him soon after, Gist as guardian and executor became the main beneficiary, but he had already acquired the land and slaves of John Smith sen. and of John Massie. As Gist noted in his defence, no challenge had been mounted at the time. It seems there were plenty of Smiths in the area, so if John jun. and Joseph had been exploited, they should have taken action against Gist. But Joseph's son was taken in by William Anderson, which means no Smith relatives were willing or able to do this. As Gist's heir, Anderson had no interest in challenging his father-in-law's behaviour.

Reade-Rootes jun. was born in 1764, the son of Martha Jacqueline Reade Rootes, widow of Thomas Reade Rootes who had died when his son was an infant. Gist's stepson Joseph Smith married Martha Jacqueline, and helped raise her son at the Smith home at Gould's Hill. Thomas Reade Rootes jun. studied law — possibly inspired by the perceived poor treatment of his stepfather by Gist — and in 1805 he challenged the English merchant's will in the Virginia Court of Chancery, by which time he had became heir apparent to both the Massie and Smith estates. In 1794 Thomas Shore sold his right in Gould's Hill to Reade Rootes, and William Anderson claimed in a letter that he had expected Reade-Rootes to either purchase Mary Anderson's life interest in the remainder or rent it from her.[23] Anderson corrected Reade-Rootes on several other property matters, which suggests he was better informed on the matter than Rootes.[24] The same letter mentions land purchased in King William County which was paid for by John Smith's estate, and again suggests the complexity of the paper trail and the impossibility of reconstructing the various pieces of it.

If this challenge had succeeded, it could have wiped out all the remaining funds, put an end to the manumission of the slaves and even forced them to be sold to pay the outstanding debts. But Reade Rootes abandoned the case in 1822 and died two years later. There were also several other disputes over credits and debts to Gist's estate, all of which had to be completed before the freedmen could be removed to new homes.

John Massie — uncle of Gist's wife Mary — left a considerable estate to John Smith sen., though there is some question as to how profitable this was, or if it was a liability instead. Smith's wife Mary became his executrix, inheriting a third of his slaves and land for life, and a fifth of his personal estate for ever. On her death, most of the slaves were to be divided between her sons. John Smith refused to make an inventory and demanded his executors did likewise. This is an extraordinary condition, and suggests his estate had been acquired under suspicious circumstances. It created huge problems, as an inheritance cannot be distributed to heirs and debts paid if the original amounts are unknown. It is thus impossible to trace how much he left his heirs, so also how much Gist acquired on his marriage to Smith's widow Mary. There is also no suggestion as to the amount of Mary's dowry which should have been kept in trust for her if she was widowed and to pass on to her heirs.

When Reade Rootes took action against Gist for his share of the Smith-Massie inheritance, he provided worrying details of Gist's behaviour. He claimed Gist had destroyed all documents which could clarify ownership and management of the various properties. A court order of 1752 demanded Gist divide the estate among Smith's heirs, but he failed to do so. This reflects the difficulties in the Smith estate itself, as already noted. Gist remained in Virginia till 1765 and had advertised his departure for a year previously, to allow debts etc. to be settled. Anyone concerned with his treatment of his stepsons had time to resolve matters while there were witnesses alive and records extant.

Gist was repeatedly ordered to settle the guardianship of Joseph and John Smith jun's estates; in 1764–5, the former became guardian of his young brother, but was unable to sort out their affairs. He only received three hundred and sixty-two pounds from Gist, who claimed the remainder had been spent maintaining his stepsons. This is impossible to confirm; if the estates were among the oldest in the region, the soil may have become depleted, and in the absence of skilled agricultural management, the land's value may have collapsed. If an estate was abandoned for even a single season, weeds and water problems could have cost a lot of money, or even ruined it, as credit on such land would be hard to find to remedy it.

Apparently John Smith jun. ran the family store in Hanover Town, which alone should have provided him, a single man, with an adequate source of income. But letters survive in which Gist criticises his management and provides advice on how best to run his business. A letter of 1768[25] advised Smith to monitor his order books and accounts to keep on top of his trade, which seems to be common sense. He advised Smith to follow the practices of his neighbours in shipping tobacco, so it seems Gist believed the young man's financial abilities were poor. He shipped a load of tobacco on the open deck of a ship without covering which seems to be utterly reckless, and probably lost most of it.[26] Gist had been his guardian, so should have trained his young charge in their family business. Or perhaps the Smith brothers had been raised as gentlemen, rather than the tough training in business that Gist had acquired before he took charge of the family business.

In 1770 Joseph Smith consulted Patrick Henry regarding his inheritance.[27] He informed Smith that, though an order had been made by the court to divide his late father's estate, no action had been taken in chancery. Henry also questioned whether his mother had renounced her husband's will and attempted to regain her dowry, i.e. the money she had brought to her marriage to Smith. Unfortunately Henry's career took off soon after, so he was unable to provide further advice.

There was also a dispute over the ownership of slaves who Gist claimed as his own. Gist claimed in a letter to Joseph that his father's will "could have no weight in any court", and that even had Smith the elder been alive and given evidence in a similar case, it "would open a door for numberless frauds".[28] Gist seems to be claiming a high level of legal knowledge, or perhaps he was trying to bully his stepson to drop the case, suggesting he had something to hide. His claim that even the best lawyers could make mistakes seems to refer to Henry, and to be daring his stepson to challenge him. But the young Smiths seem to have been out of their depth, with the only advice seeming to be from Gist, so there seems to have been a conflict of interest between himself and his wards.

This complex web of inheritances was the second case which faced Wickham in the Virginia Court of Chancery, both of which delayed the freedom and resettlement of Gist's former slaves. The only payment made by Gist as guardian to the sons of John Smith sen. was £360/18/12 to Joseph as a final settlement, in September 1765. But at this distance, it is impossible to establish whether this derisory amount reflected the low value of the Smith and the

Massie lands, or whether — as Gist claimed — his stepsons ran up such huge debts that they lost their inheritances. They may have been surviving on credit, as the rent listings for 1763 shows they owned both the estates previously owned by their father.

Thomas Reade-Rootes jun. alleged that Gist was responsible for "the strangest combination of circumstances... to enable one set of persons to deprive others of their estates".[29] He apparently saw no irony in his presence in a land stolen from native peoples by Europeans and worked by African slaves. Scattered among other sources, Gist was accused of mishandling his stepsons legacy, but he counterclaimed they were bad at running their family business, which seems to be supported by surviving letters. It seems the two generations were ill matched: the city-hardened orphan sent to survive in a strange land versus the sons of wealthy colonists who described themselves as gentlemen. Gist's letters to his stepsons show his concern for their welfare, but also his frustration at their incompetence, which put their reputations and his own at risk.

The boys grew up under the same roof as Gist before he became their guardian; this closeness should have bred close bonds between them. Gist referred to them as his sons, and his daughters as their sisters. His letters to them show paternal concern for their welfare. The boys should have been well prepared to take charge of it when they came of age, but apparently this also failed to happen. The relationship between the shop and the plantation of Gould's Hill is also unclear. Perhaps the family lived at the estate while young Gist and other servants lived at the shop to provide security in case of fire or break-in.

Details scattered through surviving letters show Gist's deep knowledge of commerce and agriculture, and a concern that his stepsons should follow the rules of business in order to survive, so accusations of exploitation do not stand up to scrutiny. A letter from Gist to his stepson John jun. claims he did not blame him for buying his brother's estate[30] which suggests Joseph was the first of the brothers to fail. Gist criticised him for buying the disputed slaves, followed by an urgent plea to forward his accounts with a list of his debts so they could be settled. Gist also complained of lack of correspondence, suggesting he knew as little of events in Virginia as in Lapland.[31]

He also cited a debt between Smith and Gist's former master or patron Lyde of about fourteen hundred pounds which caused him considerable concern, and pleaded with him to resolve the matter for his own reputation as well as for Gist's. This seems to be a desperate attempt to bail out his stepson. Gist also showed concern for his stepson's quality of life, as shown in a letter of 1768 concerning a plot of land that Smith held in Hanover Town which he suggested could be fenced and planted with apricot trees to provide shade in summer, as was the fashion in England. Gist offered to send him some of the best fruit trees and even a still to convert the fruit into brandy.[32] Such correspondence does not paint Gist as an exploiter of his stepsons.

Perhaps the Smith brothers coped when Gist was in Virginia to help them out, but once he was on the other side of the Atlantic, with letters taking months to arrive, they were left to their own devices, and so failed. Or perhaps the timing was significant. Shortly before the young men died, June 1772 saw a run on British banks, triggered by the collapse in East India Company stocks, which destabilised this huge company and its investments, but credit was probably tight for some time before this. In a region so heavily reliant on credit and loans, it is possible the Smith brothers went under while experienced dealers like Gist rode out the storm

Scattered through accounts from Virginia are numerous Smiths, yet when Joseph and John jun. died, no relatives took in Joseph's infant son, Edward Jacqueline Smith. Instead, he became ward of William Anderson.[33] The infant was Anderson's father-in-law's step grandson, a tenuous link at the best

Thomas Reade-Rootes jun. claimed to have been investigating the details of the family estates for thirty years, which begs the question why did he wait so long to mount a challenge to Gist and his representatives? He was the stepson of the late Joseph Smith who married his mother in about 1767 after she was widowed in 1763. He claimed to have found no documents relating to the Smith estate, as they had not "escaped the ravages" of Gist.[34]

After John Smith jun. died in c.1773, William Anderson became the next executor of the Smith and Massie estates, so why was this not challenged? A letter submitted to court by Reade-Rootes claimed William Anderson had sold two hundred acres of land over thirty years previously as administrator of John Smith senior's will.[35] This letter from William Burton in 1808 claimed the sale was legitimate, which raises questions about the other challenges by Reed Rootes.

Gist claimed to have a poor memory of many aspects of the challenge, which is reasonable, given the time that had elapsed since the events and his own age. But he mentioned an interesting item, that one of the Smith slaves that were in dispute was a "mulatto woman servant" with a child; her servitude was about to expire so he set them both free.[36] This incident shows Gist in a positive light and that he had form with regard to the care of his slaves, foreshadowing his later behaviour.

If the Smith sons had felt they had been exploited by their stepfather, they could have sought legal advice, or consulted their many relatives who were probably aware of what was happening, as gossip is common in all communities. But Gist's wealth gave him access to the finest legal advice in England, so they were unlikely to be successful. William Anderson, as Gist's representative, had no interest in sorting out the details. He seemed to accept that Gist's estate was legitimate, though Reade-Rootes claimed he should have known otherwise.[37] Joseph's only son was Edward Jacqueline Smith, who had been ward of William Anderson when an infant, so he must have known about the dispute but chose to ignore it. This may have been true, but Anderson had nothing to gain from annoying Gist and much to lose. As with most people involved in this story, they were all busy, living in chaotic times. They had no energy to seek out problems to solve; they were too busy coping with what fate threw at them.

William Anderson made Gist his executor when he died in

1797, so it seems whatever documents survived ended up back in the Englishman's possession. In an attempt to resolve the matter, Reade-Rootes claimed to have contacted Gist in a friendly manner to settle things. He asked for the John Smith accounts and those from his marriage to Mary until her death in 1752 when he requested Gist's accounts from the period and full details of the slaves, their names and numbers, boundaries of the five hundred acres at Goochland and much more.[38]

Gist's reply was that all matters had been settled years before, and whatever paperwork existed had long since been lost, rather than deliberately destroyed, as Reade-Rootes alleged. All of this seems reasonable. Gist had advertised for a year prior to his departure from Virginia in 1752 and again when he finally left, so such matters should have ended then. It seems he left John jun. in charge of the family business, but that he was incompetent and ran up debts with Gist and others. Gist claimed that by the time John and Joseph died, they were both in debt to him.[39] He had taken control of their father's estate and paid off all the known debts before his departure, leaving a full crop of tobacco in the business and paid three hundred and sixty-two pounds in final settlement as his duty as the executor of Smith's estate.[40]

Another source claimed Joseph owed him three hundred pounds but had been given a mill, land and tobacco.[41] Yet Gist's letters present John Smith jun. as a poor businessman, yet he had been a member of the House of Burgesses in 1772, and was a member of his local vestry and a churchwarden,[42] so he seems to have been less inept than Gist claimed. Or perhaps this highlights the huge difference between local planters and masters of the universe like Gist who played with Britain's finances in the absence of government or royal intervention.

By the time Gist's behaviour was properly challenged via the proving of his will, forty years had passed; all witnesses were dead, and even the final legatee, Reade Rootes abandoned his case for compensation in 1822.[43]

From a distance, it seem that Gist led a Midas-like existence, having started life as a poor orphan to rise up through eighteenth century society with a combination of hard work and extraordinary attention to detail. Since his master John Smith failed to provide details of his estate, it seems impossible that any challenge to Gist's management could stand up in court. It also suggests that if Gist was taking advantage of others, he was only following the lead of his former master Smith who had trained him.

Gist amassed huge wealth and he may have been an extraordinarily good businessman. But he was also fortunate enough to repeatedly find himself in the right place at the right time to make money. In an era of risk taking and gambling, perhaps being careful with his investments was the key to his success. Outliving all his peers also helped. Even if he had put all his savings in a low-interest deposit scheme, by the time he died in his tenth decade, he should have at least been living comfortably.

11

THE DESCENT OF GIST

One of the first tasks for the executors following Gist's death was to locate any heirs, especially those he named in his will. The most obvious of these was his cousin James Gist who had gone to India about forty years previously. Given that Samuel had continued his business connections with the city of his birth, and had gone there to vote in 1774 and 1781, it seems odd that he failed to inquire about James before he died. Thomas Gist, a weaver in Whitechapel attended both of these elections, so was likely a relative. Why didn't Gist track the man down? The electorate was not large; this was not a huge undertaking.

Executors placed advertisements in London and provincial papers requesting information on James or his legitimate heirs, i.e. those born in wedlock to European women, as they would inherit "considerable property, both real and personal".[1] Reasonable compensation was offered for anyone providing evidence of whether James was alive or dead. This seems to be the start of the problems, as Gist's will clearly only offered one hundred pounds to James or the same to any of his children. But James had — like so many young Britons in search of a fortune abroad — died soon after his arrival in India. Advertisements were also placed in the Virginian press calling for debtors and creditors to contact Gist's London solicitors.

On 5 March 1815 an auction was announced to dispose of Gist's property,[2] which provides an insight into the man's lifestyle. Had he been the miser that some critics claimed, it is unlikely he would have chosen a large townhouse, 37 Gower Street, with extensive stables and outbuildings, not far from the Foundling Hospital and the British Museum. It was described as containing seven public rooms including two dining rooms with folding doors, which suggests he was fond of large dinner parties. An excellent kitchen, larder and butler's room backs up this theory. It was described as "a substantial, well built family house". Yet except for a short time when his daughter Mary was a widow and lived there with her two wards, it seems Gist lived there alone with his servants, though he was such a busy man he was probably seldom at home.

A week later the contents of Gist's home were auctioned; they were suitably expensive, with plenty of mahogany furniture, chintz patterned curtains, goose feather beds and a collection of paintings which were to be sold without reserve.[3] Artists named include the forgotten or mis-spelled Weemix, as well as pieces by Le Brun and Ruysdael which suggest Gist was something of a connoisseur. But they were without frames, so had not been hung on his walls, suggesting he had acquired them as a job lot, perhaps at a bankruptcy sale or in payment of some outstanding debt.

In the succeeding years, several matters were dealt with in chancery by various heirs. Many of the details do not survive, but there is a curious item in Gist's will before he describes his manumission. He mentioned a John Wilkinson of Stockton who he owed money over "a parcel of indentured Servants consigned to William Anderson of Virginia for Sale" which was not settled at the death of Wilkinson. Gist claimed to have lost the paperwork, but allocated one hundred pounds to the man's heirs, and if this was not sufficient, then the difference was to be made good.

This Wilkinson's will was proven in November 1797,[4] so he was not the famous ironmaster who died in 1808, but they may have been related. The Stockton to Darlington Railway which opened in

1825 was the first permanent steam driven railway, so the town had similar connections with coal and steel. He was involved in colonial shipping, including the transportation of indentured servants to America, and invested in several of Samuel's ships to become very wealthy; he owned large estates in England and had been mayor of Stockton. But his long, rambling will was mostly a list of the various stocks he wished to leave to his heirs, so his financial management was similar to Gist's. It makes no mention of any dispute with Samuel, especially over one hundred pounds which would have been small change to him, so it is are unclear why the matter continued to trouble Gist. It seems Wilkinson leased ships to the British government as troop carriers when the war threatened. He had a small share in Gist's ship the Mary which arrived in Virginia; the local press claimed Gist must have been aware of Wilkinson's crime of shipping troops to North America, making himself an accessory to it.[5]

War had not broken out at the time, and ships took time to organise, so such charges seem curious. The allegation was rebutted in the press, but rumours that Gist was a traitor seem to have gained ground, as William Anderson found it impossible to get the Mary loaded in the scramble to export tobacco ahead of the outbreak of hostilities. It is very odd that the matter should have troubled Gist so many years later, especially as he seems to have lost money as a result of Wilkinson's behaviour. As with so much in this story, many details have been lost. Yet it was the last item in his will, so appears to have been an afterthought.

There was another strand to the story which appeared in the press in 1826 when Jonathan Guest or Gist of Salop Moor died; claims were made that he was a nephew of Samuel.[6] This was the John Guest who was born in 1727 so was a near contemporary of Samuel, and who had a similar gift for money making. He became involved in coal mining and iron smelting. In 1763 he leased a property in Glamorgan on the River Taff where he built a blast furnace with several investors including an Isaac Wilkinson who had established the Dowlais Works.[7] But the business struggled so they sold it to Anthony Bacon, who had established the Cyfarthfa works on another part of the river. Bacon was a former Virginian planter and colleague of Samuel Gist in the Great Dismal Swamp Company.

Bacon was born in Whitehaven, Cumbria, where George Washington, his partner in this company also had family ties.[8] Like Gist, Bacon was an orphan, and at the age of eight had been sent to Maryland. On his return, he ran his business from Throgmorton Street, so was near to the Lydes. By his death, Bacon owned three Welsh ironworks, a Cumberland coal mine and still held large estates in Maryland. He was also M.P. for Aylesbury, so was influential in promoting his own investments and businesses. His works made use of Boulton and Watt engines, which provides a link with Birmingham's Lunar Men. One of whom was Dr Joseph Priestly, the chemist and Nonconformist minister who married John Wilkinson's sister[9], so the links within the industry were many and various.

Samuel's home town of Bristol played a major role in early coal works by providing funding for the foundrymen. Samuel's master Lionel Lyde sen. had been involved in ironworks in Virginia. Abraham Darby failed to gain support in the city, but when he moved to Coalbrookdale, he died before his sons were old enough to inherit. His fellow Quakers the Goldney family of Bristol helped maintain the company. William Reynolds (1735–1816) another near contemporary of Samuel's married into the Darby family whose works produced the world's first iron railway line. He became a major benefactor of his home city, establishing a bank for the poor. Latimer called him "the greatest of Bristol's benefactors".[10] He officially distributed £200,000 to the city, including rebuilding part of the Infirmary, but he allegedly gave much more privately.[11] This raises questions as to whether Gist also made private donations to good causes.

John Guest became the manager of the huge Dowlais Works, his son followed him and by 1851 was in sole control of it. Their company expanded as the railway age created huge demand for iron tracks, including the Stockton to Darlington railway which opened in 1825. They virtually held a monopoly on the iron business, with customers including the Navy Board, East India Company and governments across the globe, from the USA to China. John Guest's son became a baronet and left the family business in trust for his children. It became GKN (Guest Keen & Nettlefolds) which is the oldest engineering firm in Britain.[12] The similarity of their names, and the timing of the deaths of the very wealthy Gist and Guest seem to have created understandable confusion, and probably a scramble to claim inheritances from both men.

These patterns of similar names, these parallels between Samuel and the Guests of the Welsh coal and ironmasters are too numerous to be random, especially given the relative rarity of Gist and other names. Gist's American connection with Bacon, the repeated linkage between the name Guest/Gist and Wilkinson seems too much of a coincidence. The ironmaster John Guest employed an ironmaster from his home of Broseley named John Onions.[13] In Gist's will he mentions a man named Onions who married his mother's sister. The Lyde family were from North Somerset, which seems to set them apart, but the area was part of a large coal field which provided the raw materials for industries in the area.

There also seems to be a repeating pattern of links with the River Severn, which allowed northerners to seek out new sources of coal and iron, and to use the great river to transport it. The first properties Gist bought in England seem to have been Wormington, Dixton and Dumbleton, all within reach of the lower part of the River Severn. The Savage family who are buried near him in Wormington church arrived there from northern counties, and were also linked with the North American colonies. This seems to suggest Samuel Gist's family may likewise have originated in northern woodlands. Was he accepted into Queen Elizabeth's Hospital on the basis that his father John trained in Bristol, rather than was born there? Did Samuel invest in some of these ventures, encouraging the investigation and foundations of them? Isaac Wilkinson's life was described as largely itinerant, so how did he fund his travels to investigate sources of underground wealth?

Though Josiah Sellick became Gist's main heir he had to wait till Mary and Elizabeth died to inherit the full amount. In the meantime, he was provided with an annual allowance of five hundred pounds. But the codicil in the will altered this, so he received only three hundred pounds per year. Gist's daughters received the income from all his English lands; on the death of Elizabeth, her share went to Mary, on whose death the full legacy went to Josiah. It is unknown how Sellick passed his time in the interim; even three hundred pounds per year was a comfortable sum to live on. It is also unclear why he chose Wormington Grange as his family home, especially as it was in breach of Samuel's wishes. But by then there were no family members to challenge him, and the executors were probably exhausted.

Gist's long, rambling will has generated misunderstandings and erroneous claims on both sides of the Atlantic, especially in relation to the fate of his great wealth. One of the many errors repeated is that the daughters opposed the manumission of the slaves and tried to block the process. But soon after Gist's will was proven in England, Martin and Mary Pearkes and William and Elizabeth Fowkes petitioned the Virginia Assembly to free the slaves, as per their father's will. It was then agreed that it was "just and proper" to honour this aspect of the will. This largely ended the Gist family's involvement in Virginia. Though Elizabeth and Mary had been praised by the slaves for their kindness, there is no evidence they took any further interest in their welfare.

Samuel's will clearly stated his English wealth was not to be used to pay for any American debts, but as all his wealth there was to be put to the use of his freed slaves, this was the only source of funding any challenges, as subsequently happened with the two court cases mentioned earlier.

Gist's daughters could have challenged the manumission, and continued to receive the profits of the estates, especially as technically some of them belonged to Mary and it is unclear what happened to the land she was left by her husband's will. This may have been the basis for the Anderson challenge, which should have been fought out in the London court.

Mary and Elizabeth had led comfortable lives, and were well provided for by their father's will, especially Mary. They received all the profits of their father's lands till the last of them died, which was more than enough to live comfortably. William Anderson's will included a wish that his slaves should be given to his mother on his death, and on her decease, they were to be freed. He also requested they be treated kindly, so he and his wife may have provided the inspiration for Samuel's decision to manumit his own slaves. It was easier for both men to free their slaves than for those who still lived in Virginia. They had other sources of income, and they did not have to deal with the after effects of their decisions.

By the time Samuel died, both his daughters were also advanced in years. Both had received income from Gist's plantations throughout their lives, and it seems their husbands had run successful businesses, though Anderson had spent too much time taking orders from Gist to devote his life to an independent career. They had little need for money to see out their final years. If he doubted his daughters' support for the manumission, Samuel could have freed the slaves before he died, but the war intervened. He wished the slaves to continue working to generate income for his daughters until they were freed. He had kept in touch with attorney John Wickham who continued to collect debts for him, but Gist seems not to have consulted him regarding the manumission

The timing of Gist's manumission is also significant, as the slave trade had been abolished in England between Gist writing his will and his death, so he and Anderson were possibly following the public mood at the time. Gist offered Mary two thousand pounds per year for surrendering her interest in the plantations, plus fifteen hundred pounds annually to replace the five hundred pounds per year she had been paid to renounce her claims on the properties her husband William Anderson had bought for Gist during the Revolutionary War. If the manumission was refused, Gist intended the slaves to be kept working, and if there was insufficient land to occupy the growing numbers, then more land was to be purchased and his daughters were to receive the profits. Yet again, Gist showed his objection to idleness, reflecting his own long lifetime of hard work.

᪥

Despite Gist's immense wealth, he is almost invisible in historic records. His huge donation of ten thousand pounds to Queen Elizabeth's Hospital was his largest, but even it was poorly planned. In 1820 a charity in his name was established in his name, funded by government stocks which produced 3% per year to support six each of poor men, poor women, boys and girls. But the institution was for boys only, which Gist must have known, so this suggests whoever wrote the will knew nothing about the school, so this bequest was problematic from the outset. Also, the funds were insufficient for his proposals from the beginning, so the matter had to be resolved in the Court of Chancery, causing it to be delayed. Eventually, the legacy was adapted to fund three boys at Gist's former school, and to fund their apprentice fees, for three girls at the sister school of Red Maids' and for six shillings per week to be given to three poor men and five shillings per week to three poor women.

After the passage of the Municipal Corporations Act of 1835 the charity was absorbed into the Bristol Municipal Charities. Queen Elizabeth's Hospital funds were sometimes plundered by the corporation, in its early days, and the practice seems to have continued. A local newspaper of 1840 cited hundreds of pounds being spent by a number of charities in legal fees. It claimed some of Gist's charity was spent on road money, i.e. repairs.[14] And yet in 1871 a new scheme was announced from London for rearrangements of the six charity schools in Bristol including Queen Elizabeth's Hospital which involved taking money from local educational charities. Twenty thousand pounds was to be taken from the Peloquin Gift which had been left by a Huguenot family and smaller sums from others including Samuel Gist's,[15] which suggests his legacy had been well invested and increased considerably. The Samuel Gist Educational Charity was listed with the Bristol Municipal Charities, but removed from the register as it ceased to exist on 17 March 2015, when its funds ceased to exist. Had he left land to Queen Elizabeth's Hospital instead of stocks, its value would have more than kept pace with inflation, but it would also have needed management, which was beyond the remit of subsequent administrators.

William Anderson, who had managed Gist's affairs in Virginia and had cared for Gist's step-grandson/half brother-in-law John Smith, and protected the Englishman's lands from confiscation, must have longed for the day when he would be rewarded with a huge inheritance, but this was not to be. By 1790 he was claimed to be the largest tobacco importer in London, in partnership with William Fowkes. But in September 1795 he must have been dying as Anderson wrote his will at Chesterfield. He had travelled there with his wife, sister-in-law and others in hope of a cure, but he died there the following 1 January. He and his wife had been living at the red-brick Belmont House in Vauxhall, now on Nine Elms Lane. It was subdivided and the Anderson's lived in the smaller part, but it was sold in 1811 to Wilhelm, Duke of Brunswick.[16] The couple may have moved there seeking fresh air for Anderson's failing health.

He left his wife all the properties in Virginia including their former home, the Dundee Plantation, and the estates which Gist had vested in her in 1782 and all their household furniture etc, during her life, and assumed care would be taken to provide for their adopted children. On her death, their home was to be given to his nephew Francis Anderson. All the property he had purchased for Gist from the executors of John Bickerton in Hanover County of about six hundred acres and about two thousand two hundred acres formerly owned by Thomas Massie, in Goochland were to go to his father-in-law on condition he pay the purchase price and interest within twelve months. The land was not to be divided, possibly to ensure all the slaves working the plantations were kept together. If Gist refused to pay, the properties were to be sold and the executors were to demand the interest and rents that Gist had received. Anderson also ordered the sale of the land in Albermarle County which he had inherited from his grandfather. This may have been the land which his relatives claimed when they challenged the Gist manumission, as some restriction may have existed to control it leaving the family. Despite this, he still referred to Gist as "his worthy friend" rather than father-in-law. He used the same term for his other executor William Fowkes, his brother-in-law.

William's main heir was his nephew Francis Anderson who was to receive all his possessions not left to his wife, and funding to learn a trade when he came of age at twenty-two. This is a curiosity as apprenticeships were generally for teenagers who qualified around the age of twenty-one or at the end of their term. It seems young gentlemen were given more time for their education — including travel such as going on the Grand Tour — before embarking on a career and marriage. If he died before coming of age, then his inheritance was to go to his cousin Maria Gist Anderson. Both William's wards were left to the care of Gist. Anderson wished all his slaves to be treated kindly and left to his mother and on her death to be freed.

But William's nephew and heir did not long survive him. Described as a gentleman, he wrote his will on 28 April 1800 when he was living at Paddington Green. This was a leafy village within easy reach of London. He had turned twenty-two the previous December, so inherited a large part of his late uncle's estate, but it had not yet been divided so he left his share to his cousin Maria Gist who was living with their aunt, William's widow Mary at Samuel's house at 37 Gower Street. Francis left one hundred pounds to Mrs Anne Beresford, a widow who was probably nursing the young invalid. He died about six months later. Thus a large part of William Anderson's wealth in Virginia descended to Maria Gist Anderson.

❧

The little information which survives about Gist's heirs comes largely from their wills. His youngest daughter Elizabeth Fowke seldom appeared in records. Several times in American documents her sister Mary was described as an only child, suggesting she was more active in social circles, or — more likely — because she had returned to live in Virginia for several years, so was more visible via her involvement in property and business there. Elizabeth wrote her will in February 1819 and died the following year. Her address was "Brightonstown" in Sussex, the seaside town and modern hipster centre of Brighton where she may have gone for her health. She was also "sometime resident" at Chelworth House where she died on 22 March 1820 at the age of sixty-six.[17]

With her elder sister, she shared the rental income from Gist's extensive property portfolio in the counties of Gloucestershire, Oxfordshire, Warwickshire and Worcester, invested in interest-generating government consols. This may have been to save them the trouble of managing the various estates, they were popular with people who dealt in stocks and shares and were a major source of finance for the many wars which shored up Britain's economy. She named her husband, William, a former naval officer and subsequently a tobacco trader, as executor, as was George Fowke of Sible-hedingham, Essex — probably her brother-in-law, who served in the navy. In 1801 a load of Honduras mahogany was advertised for sale from the Triton, which had been captured by George Fowkes, captain of the H.M. Proselyte.[18] Soon after, another of George's prizes, the brig Proteus and its cargo including wool, Swedish iron, barrels of fish and twenty-eight hogsheads of tobacco were auctioned.[19] So he was a successful officer.

Elizabeth left money to her husband's relatives, and annual sums to her husband's niece and to her maid. Women tended to be more in need of such inheritances as so few professions were open to them at the time, and they were lowly paid. If single or widowed, they often descended into poverty without such assistance. Her jewellery, including a locket containing the hair of a friend, was distributed among female friends and relatives, and her pianoforte was left to a Mary Fidor with a legacy. This suggests that the passing mention of Gist's daughter playing the piano for Patrick Henry[20] was her. In 1826 her widowed husband married the widow Anna Maria Waring, the only daughter of Job Hanmer, R.N.[21] He died three years later at Great Saling, Essex aged eighty-five.[22]

In February 1819 Martin Pearkes wrote his will which was proven in January 1821. He died at Upper Harley Street at the age of seventy-six.[23] His origins are not clear, but Gist had traded with a tobacconist called Parks from Bristol, so he was probably yet another member of this transatlantic merchant circle. He had been in business with William Anderson, and his family name can be found in Temple Parish in Bristol. He was likely in the tobacco business for some time, so Mary's remarriage may have been in part to continue her husband's business. But in William Anderson's will, Pearkes held all of Gist's Virginia lands on behalf of his wife, as she could not legally own them. She regained them on his death, as widows had equal rights to property as men, but when she married Pearkes, they were transferred to him.

Like Gist, he was involved in charities, but on a much smaller scale. He served as a steward for the Smallpox and Inoculation Hospital and gave money to the poor of his parish of Marylebone.[24] His will is largely free of legal jargon, and seems to have been penned by himself, as there are moments of wry humour scattered through it. He allowed Mary the use of all crockery etc, wishing her to keep them in good order, "ordinary casualties excused". Was this a private joke between them? He left his widow all the silver plate which she had inherited from her first husband and her father, as well as books, bookcases, maps, prints and paintings from them. He confirmed her ownership of various pieces of jewellery, watches and trinkets, as well as carriages, harnesses etc. This is another reminder of the property rights of women at the time, but that many husbands honoured them nonetheless.

He left her their home and its contents, and another on Grove Place, near Lissom Grove in Marylebone, London. He provided legacies to his sister Mary Pearkes, to Elizabeth and Martin Fowkes, and to his niece Elizabeth Gundry and daughter Carolina Pearkes Weatherall, so, like Mary Gist, they were both on their second marriages. His wife was to receive one hundred pounds per year, and fifty pounds annually going to his wife's heir, Maria Gist Anderson, the orphaned niece of William Anderson who had by then married William Beddis. He provided cash for mourning rings, and several houses owned by him in Newgate were to provide income for his nieces. Finally, he wished to be buried in St James' Chapel, Regent's Park in Marylebone.

This little-known church is significant, as it served the local American community. Despite all their years spent in London, they were part of a small community of expatriates, possibly marginalised for continuing to make money from slavery when the abolition movement was attracting so much support in Britain. The following March, the lease of the "very desirable house"[25] with coach house and stables was sold at the 'low' rent of £180 per year.

On 28 February 1822, Gist's last surviving daughter died. Mary Gist Anderson Pearkes' will was written in January 1822 and was proven the following April. She had acquired her sister's share of the money left to compensate them for abandoning any claims to the Virginia properties and slaves. As it was in stock, she divided it between her heirs, two thirds of it going to her heir and step-niece, Maria Gist Beddis, specifically for her own use, and the rest to Maria's husband William Beddis. On her niece's death, the funds were to go to their daughters, Mary Elizabeth Beddis and Francis Maria in equal shares; if their father should interfere, he was to lose his share, so attempts were made to ensure the financial security of the young girls, though again, this was not likely to stand up to any court challenge. That said, any challenge would likely have been held up in the black hole of the Court of Chancery, thus providing a further incentive to agree to the terms.

Mary also bequeathed to her niece the one thousand two hundred pounds from her marriage settlement which William Anderson had provided, derived from Virginia properties. This is confusing as claims were made the couple lived in poverty when they returned to Virginia after their marriage. She passed on items such as miniatures of her sister and brother-in-law and a portable writing desk, and she left to William Fowkes, the former naval officer, a painting of the Port of Cadiz. To her niece she left a portrait of Samuel Gist in oil, which is intriguing, but as no artist was named, this is unlikely to be traceable. She also left miniatures of herself and William Anderson and her choice of books, prints, etc. She was buried with her husband in the American chapel vault. Samuel Gist had a reputation among the North Americans for being a difficult man, a miser and worse. But from the above, it seems his daughters seem to have married well and left heirs that they cared about. Samuel must had raised them well.

We are in the dark as to how to where Josiah Sellick lived between the death of Samuel and becoming the lord of the manor of Wormington Grange. He quickly changed his name to Gist under the terms of Samuel's will and he became entitled to three hundred pounds per year and the death of Mary when he received the lion's share of Gist's estate at last. From 1826–8 he employed Henry Hakewell to enlarge and decorate Wormington Grange, along similar lines to his Stisted Hall in Essex of 1823.

But this was not what Gist had intended. His will clearly stated that he wished the house to be converted into a school for poor boys. Why did the executors not permit this? Perhaps Gist had not allocated enough funds, but there was plenty of money which could have been diverted for this purpose, and several other properties — especially nearby Dixton — which Josiah Gist could have made his home. But a newspaper account describes the estate. It was described as being beautifully situated in woodland, a mansion in five hundred acres which included a large lake. An oak room included an oak suite from the time of Edward VI and several paintings including a depiction of Queen Elizabeth visiting his other estate at Dixton.[26]

In September 1814 Josiah Sellick was named as one of the builders and part owner of the Princess Charlotte of Bristol, with the Hillhouse family who had been trading with North America for over a century, so he was moving in similar circles to those of his late patron.[27] In December 1815 he was one of the owners who sold the ship. After his name it was noted that he had assumed the name of Gist. The remaining share of the ship was sold in January 1823. Josiah Sellick (1765–1834)[29] had a son who died at the age of fourteen in 1806.[28]

But as Josiah Gist seems to have discovered, wealth does not buy access to polite society. In 1824 Josiah was described by local parson Rev. Wells as a 'rich parvenu'.[30] His eldest son, Samuel Gist Gist, had married Mary Anne Westenra, the only daughter of Lord Rossmore, who lived nearby. The doubling of his surname is odd, as it suggests his mother had been a Gist, which seems impossible, but given how curious Gist's life had been, this cannot be ruled out. But marrying into the aristocracy offered little advancement, as she was described by the same cleric as amiable but lacking in talent and beauty, though he conceded the young couple seemed happy together. A month later the parson's opinion of the family improved when they had invited his mother to stay for several weeks. He described their mansion as comfortable but not handsome, which is probably why they had it improved by Hakewell. The same Samuel had a museum of natural curiosities which included objects from the South Seas.

In 1834 Josiah became High Sheriff of Gloucestershire, an honour which involved great expense in providing dinners for other officers. In the summer he presided over a dinner in Gloucester, attended by the governors of the Gloucester Infirmary who remained in town to attend the summer assizes. But Josiah began drinking early — apparently not unusual for him; he arrived in town in a state of excitement and behaved in a depraved and vulgar manner. The dinner was not attended by a great number of men, but they were well behaved. Josiah later rambled in the street, swearing until late at night, and stormed around the hotel, shouting and swearing. He died soon after.[31]

Josiah's son Samuel Gist Gist inherited Wormington Grange, his other son William rented a property called Dove Dale at the entrance of Blockley estate, owned by Lord North in 1838.[32]

The final record of this generation of the family was at the funeral of Lady Rossmore, Samuel's sister-in -law. At the funeral conducted by Rev. Wells of Cheltenham, he met Gist and a relative of the Lord, but he noted that some of the mourners could not be identified as relatives or servants of the Gists, so again suggesting the family had not established a local presence. Lord Rossmore had no male heir, so the title died with him, but the family name survived when one of the Gist children added the Irish family name to his, with Samuel's youngest son becoming Henry Westenra Gist.

The Gist estate seems to have been largely run down during the next generation when the eldest son of Samuel Gist, Samuel Gist Gist was declared a lunatic in 1853 at the age of twenty-one years. He lived for many years at Wormington Grange, as well as owning estates at Evesham and lands in Oxfordshire and Gloucestershire. His brother was the above Henry Westenra Gist. Samuel Gist was described as being of unsound mind, with weak faculties and incapable of caring for himself since the death of his father.[33] This seems to suggest the death of his father was so traumatic as to cause such severe mental health problems, which seems unlikely. He died in April 1904 after a long illness. His brother Henry Westenra Gist died in June 1920 at Alstone Manor, apparently the last of Samuel Gist's male descendants. Miss Du Pre, their niece seems to have been the last of the Gist descendants to live at Wormington Grange where she had been with her sister for many years.[34]

12

GIST'S LEGACY

S amuel Gist's story has intrigued this author for many years. The rise of an orphan to become one of the richest and most benevolent men of his age seems to fit more with fiction than fact. Whilst his long-term legacy to the descendants of his slaves continues to be debated, his lifetime achievements were impressive.

But like good fiction, we are still left with many unanswered — and intriguingly unanswerable —questions, especially regarding his motives. He must have been a man of strong will, of great physical and mental endurance, merely to have survived into his tenth decade. But running through his career seems to have been a goal which continues to elude researchers. Though he had no grandchildren of his own bloodline, his eldest daughter seems to have had two successful marriages and been devoted to her adopted niece and nephew, and his younger daughter had a long and successful marriage. Samuel had amassed enough money to have retired and spent his later years as a doting father and grandfather. Yet he continued to appear on the Exchange, continued to buy and manage properties. It seems that whatever had driven him to build his wealth was still part of him. Like Midas, it seems, his hunger for acquiring wealth was insatiable.

Gist's reason for freeing his slaves may have been to provide a living community to remember him. Though most of the land has sadly been lost, the final community, in Highland Country, has recently ensured its future, thanks in large part to the long battle by a descendant of the freedmen, Paul Turner. After a long career in the navy he campaigned and invested much of his savings in trying to keep the land. Other descendants of the freed slaves have pursued justice in various courts, though with little success. But descendants of the various settlers have been gathering to share their stories and discuss their shared history, so perhaps this is ultimately Samuel's legacy.

With no images of Gist, we are still left to imagine this intriguing but mysterious man. In some ways he resembles modern magnates, especially several in the media who are only being prodded towards retirement — or at least a withdrawal from the front lines of their empires — by the unstoppable march of modern media. For some, it seems the reins of power will only be removed from their hands after they have breathed their last.

When Elizabeth I ordered the final abolition of Catholic practices, this was strictly enforced. She wanted more than an end to the ancient rituals, she demanded their extirpation. Stone coffins were converted to animal troughs and baptismal fonts used as pig feeders, which suggests they had been large. Babies were immersed in cold water not just to confirm their admission into the religious community, but to test their stamina. Tough times allow little room for sentimentality. Claims have been made that children of a harsh winter are more robust than the norm, as they learn to fight for survival from the outset. Perhaps this was the key to Gist's success. Maybe as an orphan in a tough port city, he leapt from the starting blocks ahead of his peers and kept on going.

But an orphan needed to forge bonds for support and advice. Though parallels have been drawn between his early career and that of Lyonel Lyde jun., in their work experience in Virginia, Gist lacked Lyde's safety net, i.e. his family, to provide advice on business and financial matters. Both men married and were widowed in Virginia, but Lyde remarried and produced several more sons when he returned to England, whereas Samuel remained a widower. Lyde also ran a business with his brother, whereas Gist seems to have been a sole trader throughout his life.

All this helps explain how Samuel amassed his money. He seems to have enjoyed the male environment on the Exchange and the various coffee houses. He left to his daughter Mary a dinner service with his coat of arms on it, so he must have enjoyed large-scale entertaining, and we cannot see him as some solitary miser. Yet we are still left with the mystery of what drove him. Perhaps it reflected his age, when life for everyone was a full of risks, so a gambling culture was part of this. Investment in stocks and shares was a grand game which could make a fortune overnight. This can be seen in lives of the great explorers such as William Dampier. Despite being one of the greatest explorers and navigators of his age, he died in obscurity, his legacy overshadowed by the likes of Cook and Bligh.

Perhaps Gist's will provides the key. There is an item that other authors seem to have missed, or to have misunderstood the significance of. Gist kept a marble coffin in his stables at Gower Street where he died in London, which seems strange, given his intention to be buried at the church on his estate of Wormington Grange in Gloucestershire. When this author discussed this matter with friends, the most usual response was to ask if he ever tried it out for size, that perhaps he was an ancestor of modern Goths.

But he was a man of common sense. He had clearly been preparing for his death, as the Grim Reaper must have been getting frustrated by the time he finally made his appearance. When the founder of Queen Elizabeth's Hospital, John Carr, died in 1586, he left five shillings to repair the family tomb in St Werburgh's, one of the richest parishes, in the centre of Bristol. He requested that after his death, and those of his wife and sister, the vault "should never be opened until the world's end".[1]

St Katherine's churchyard, Wormington, Gloucestershire

Gist wished to be buried in the church of St Katherine on his estate, and left instructions to open up the crypt and build steps into it for his admission, which meant he would be the first person for centuries to be interred there. In death, as in much of his life, he would be alone. Which is again unusual. Most people preferred to rest surrounded by friends and family for company at the Resurrection. The church register shows he was buried on 28 January 1825 but incorrectly states he was ninety years old.

Yet he did not order a grand memorial to himself, as was common at the time. A simple plaque of local bluestone was to be fixed on the north wall of the chancel. He could have recorded his many benefactions to charities, as did Edward Colston. It seems there would be nobody in the church who knew him or who would pray for his soul apart from his adopted family, the Sellicks, several generations of whom later joined him.

But on the south wall of the chancel , facing him across the altar is a larger, bluestone classical monument commemorating his son-in-law William Anderson, with space for his wife's details to be added, though he had made no mention of any burial plans in his will. They had caused each other a lot of pain, but at the end they found peace, in a rather Georgian, manly kind of way.

Samuel Gist's monument on the north side of the chancel of St Katherine's church, Wormington, Gloucestershire.

Perhaps the church was chosen for its name. St Katherine was patron saint of weavers, so hugely important to the West Country, and a fine chapel was dedicated to her in Temple Parish in Bristol which Samuel probably knew from his childhood. John Wesley preached in the church, and described it as 'the most beautiful ancient church in Bristol'.[2]

When the traditional system of fair prices for food in open markets broke down from the mid-eighteenth century, the weavers were in the forefront of rioting. But these were not ordinary riots; they often confronted farmers on their way to market, asked them what price they demanded, and if it was too high, the mob took the grain and sold it at a fair price which was handed on to the farmers. The region had also been prominent in tobacco growing, and rioting against its suppression to ensure high prices for Virginia planters, so the parish and the region had many points of contact with Gist's life and career.

William Anderson's monument, St Katherine's Church, Wormington, Gloucestershire

The most noteworthy memorial in St Katherine's is a brass plaque commemorating Anne Savage and her infant from 1605. She was apparently a member of the "Cotswold Savages", whose husband was from Norbury in Worcester, a large family that included Captain Anthony Savage (1605–95) who was born at nearby Broadway and died at Jamestown, Gloucester Country in Virginia. They were described as "one of the first families of Virginia".[3] A number of Savage graves survive in surrounding parish registers, where several Guests can also be found, one of whom was married by licence, meaning they were wealthy. It is possible he two families were intermarried.

Wormington Grange, Wormington, Gloucestershire.

Wormington was the first of Samuel's purchases; the house was built in the 1770s by Nathaniel Jeffries who had purchased the land and manorial rights. Gist purchased it in 1787 when he was listed as a Bristol merchant. So it seems he still felt close links with the West Country. The Lyde family and most other London merchants built country estates within commuting distance of the capital, so yet again, Gist was bucking the fashions. But it is unclear what he used it for, as he seems to have made no improvements to the old house. At the time of his death the estate was rented to Joseph Wheeler, so Gist did not use it as a country retreat or for his retirement.

Buried within his will is the key to this important purchase. Unnoticed by other researchers is his request for the house to be converted to a school, allocating twenty pounds per year for its master, funded by one thousand pounds of 3% consols, to provide books, pens, paper etc. any surplus was to be used for clothes.[4]

Is this the crucial, missing part of the Gist puzzle? His rise to success and great wealth was only possible because of the benefactions of John Carr. As a student he must have been well aware of his good fortune, and with his fellows, have prayed for the merchant's soul. Was this Gist's way of acknowledging and of passing on his good fortune so that other poor boys would be given a chance at a better life?

It is unclear why this bequest was ignored. In 1826-8, after the death of Samuel's last daughter, Josiah Gist —formerly Sellick — inherited the bulk of Gist's huge wealth. He employed the architect Henry Hakewell to enlarge Wormington Grange and extensively redecorate it as his family home, providing a base for him to join the gentry of Gloucestershire.[5]

There is another Bristol benefactor whose life may have inspired him, and who was also involved in the slave trade, via his membership of the Royal Africa Company. Edward Colston was born into a Bristol merchant family in the parish of Temple, which may also have been Gist's birthplace. His life is poorly documented, but one source claimed he lived in Spain with his father and two brothers, so like Gist learned about commerce from abroad. The Colstons seem to have been heavily involved in importing wine etc. from the region, and a source claims his brothers were poisoned, which left him as an only child, again like Gist.[6] Another source claims cites the man himself, saying that he was educated and spent most of his life in London.

Like Gist, he was also long lived and when he died aged eighty-four at Mortlake in 1721 he was buried in his family's former parish of All Saints. Also like Gist, his coffin had travelled for several days, during which bystanders would have learned of the great man and perhaps prayed for his soul. Colston's large monument is by Rysbrack and records his many charitable bequests, for him to be remembered as a good Christian. His motto was said to have been inspired by the Good Samaritan, *Go thou and do likewise*, and he is claimed to have set standards in charity that inspired future Bristolians. His will provided mourning clothes for the many beneficiaries of the charities he had established, from two schools and two almshouses, who met the hearse at Lawford's Gate and escorted it through pouring rain to his interment at around midnight. Parish church bells tolled for a migraine-inducing sixteen hours.

Gist was not born at the time, but this funeral was unprecedented in its pomp and scale, and Queen Elizabeth's Hospital was funded in part by Colston during and after his lifetime. Colston had survived the Civil War and referred to Cromwell as 'the Usurper', so was a strict Tory and a High Church Anglican, so refused to support Nonconformists, which meant that further donations were diverted elsewhere. Gist's will insisted his slaves be instructed in the Church of England, but there is nothing to suggest he went to church himself. He left no legacies to any groups that were primarily religious.

Like Gist, Colston's huge wealth targeted specific causes which were close to the merchant's hearts. Pre-Reformation, donations were for people to pray for the donor's soul to reduce their time in purgatory. A passing bell was rung when a wealthy parishioner died to encourage those within hearing to pray to relieve their suffering in passing from this world. Neither Colston nor Gist lived in the parish where they were buried, so the legacies were realised after they died.

Gist wanted to be in the church where the schoolboys prayed; his name clearly on the wall to remind them that he was responsible for their education and protection from poverty. But also for his life to provide an example to them that it was possible to overcome a difficult beginning to succeed in a harsh, unstable world.

He also commissioned a hatchment representing his family name. The motto displayed could not be more appropriate: RESURGAM, to rise, or endure. Gist's family name is an ancient English one meaning stranger or —more obviously — a guest.

It is unknown why Wormington Grange was not converted to use as a school. Josiah Gist inherited several estates, but this was the closest to his home of Bristol which may have made it the most attractive. Perhaps Gist had not left enough funds to establish and run the school. Or perhaps Josiah liked the estate.

As a book reviewer suggested, in reference to the freeing of his slaves: "perhaps it was one last, supreme gesture of contempt towards the Virginians who had made him rich and whom he despised."[7]

Gist family hatchment, vestry, St Katherine's church, Wormington, Gloucestershire.

Many histories of the freed slaves claim that Gist's intention was for their heirs to become his living legacy, remember him, perhaps even to say prayers in his memory, which is possible. Gist's times were unstable; he saw wars, fires, famines. He outlived his peers and most of his family, not by joining the boom and bust economy that ruined so many, but by careful management, standing firm when those around him were losing their heads. He endured, and perhaps that was the most important thing.

But given his childhood, his most important legacy was the one that his heirs denied him. He had wished to found a refuge for children like he had been, for them to find shelter from a harsh world and to give thanks to his memory. They would continue the cycle of hard work and giving thanks by giving something back. They would sit in the church above the crypt where Gist slept for eternity, and when they were bored with the droning of a long sermon they might look up at the north wall and wonder about the man responsible for their presence there. And perhaps one or more of them may have been inspired to follow in his footsteps, in the traditions of Carr, Colston and many other benefactors of Protestant England.

For a man whose legacy seems to present him as a man of two seemingly irreconcilable extremes, i.e. a monster and a benefactor, there is a pleasing sense of balance and unity in the idea that two communities, of different races, on opposite sides of the Atlantic, could be praying for his soul while his mortal remains mouldered beneath the soil of the beautiful Cotswolds. It seems a perfect place for this enigmatic man to find peace. For his memory to endure.

APPENDIX I: NOTES

Introduction

1 pp. 591–2, Beers, W.H., *The History of Brown County, Ohio*, W.H. Beers, Chicago, 1883

2 Ayres, E.J., Highland Pioneer Sketches and Family Genealogies, Springfield, Ohio, 1971

3 p. 731, ditto

4 p. 732, ditto

5 p. 733, ditto

Ch. 1 Bristol

1 p. 291, Hutton, E., *Highways & Byways in Gloucestershire*, Macmillan, London, 1932

2 p. 143, Nichols, J.F., and Taylor, J., Bristol Past and Present, J.W. Arrowsmith, Bristol, 1882

3 p. 186, Grey Graham, H., *The Social Life of Scotland in the Eighteenth Century*, A&C Black Ltd, London, 1937

4 p. 470, Latimer, J., *Annals of Bristol Eighteenth Century, Vol. 2 Eighteenth Century*, George's, Bristol, 1970

5 p. 274 Trevelyan, G.M., *English Social History: A Survey of Six Centuries Chaucer to Queen Victoria*, The Reprint Society, London, 1944

6 p. 326, ditto

7 p. 201, ditto

8 p. 202, ditto

9 p. 203, ditto

10 p. 195, ditto

11 Raleigh, History of the World IV, II, 4 in p. 55 Robinson, C.N., The British Tar in Fact and Fiction, Harper and Brothers, London 1911

12 p. 226, Nichols, J.F. and Taylor, J.

13 p. 81, Latimer J.

14 p. 700, Barratt, W., *The History and Antiquities of the City of Bristol,* W. Pine, Bristol, 1789

15 p. 702, ditto

16 pp. 166–7, Latimer, J.

17 p. 290, Trevelyan, G.M.

18 pp. 8, Bowen, F.W.E., *Queen Elizabeth's Hospital, Bristol The City School,* Clevedon Printing, Clevedon, 1971

19 p. 7, ditto

20 p.75-7, Latimer, J.

21 Newcastle Courant, 6 September 1766

22 p. 11, Latimer, J.

23 p. 12, Bowen F.W.E

24 p. 31, Barratt, W.

25 p. 492, Latimer, J.

26 p. 493, ditto

Ch. 2 Samuel

1 Queen Elizabeth's Hospital Accounts Book, Bristol Record Office 33041/4

2 p. 118, Laslett, P., *The World We Have Lost Further Explored,* Taylor and Francis, London, 2001

3 p. 201, Jordan, D., and Walsh, M., *White Cargo: The Forgotten History of Britain's White Slaves in America,* Mainstream, Edinburgh, 2007

4 p. 120, Laslett, P.

5 p. 52, Reed Stiles, H., *Bundling: Its Origin, Progress and Decline in America,* Book Collectors Association, New York, 1914

6 p. 40, Bowen, F.W.E., *Queen Elizabeth's Hospital, Bristol: The City School*, Clevedon Printing, Clevedon, 1971

7 p. 43. ditto

8 Queen Elizabeth's Hospital Accounts Book

9 pp. 204–6, Latimer, J., *Annals of Bristol, Vol. 1 Seventeenth Century*, George's, Bristol, 1970

10 p. 148, Latimer, J., *Annals of Bristol Vol. 2 Eighteenth Century*, George's, Bristol, 1970

11 ditto

12 *Virginia Gazette* 25 February 1773

Ch. 3 Virginia

1 p. 150, Latimer, J., *Annals of Bristol Eighteenth Century, Vol. 1 Seventeenth Century*, George's, Bristol, 1970

2 p. 149, ditto

3 p. 34, Sale, K., *The Conquest of Paradise: Christopher Columbus and the Columbian Legacy*, Penguin, London, 1991

4 Lienhard, J.H., *Engines of Ingenuity* no. 123, The Black Death, www.uh.edu/engines/ei123.htm

5 p. 211, Trevelyan, G.M., *English Social History: A survey of Six Centuries, Chaucer to Queen Victoria*, The Reprint Society, London, 1944

6 p. 83, Jordan, D., and Walsh, M., *White Cargo: The Forgotten History of Britain's White Slaves in America*, Mainstream, Edinburgh, 2007

7 p. ix, Hayes Phillips, R., *Without Indentures: Index to White Slave Children in Colonial Court Records [Maryland and Virginia]*, Genealogical Publishing, 2013

8 p 85, Jordan, D. and Walsh

9 Donne, J., *Elegie: Going to Bed*, in p. 258 Sale, K.

10 p. xi, Dame Paul, J.W, *Bristol Privateers and Ships of War*, J.W.Arrowsmith, Bristol, 1930

11 p. 84, Jordan, D. and Walsh, M.

12 *Jackson's Oxford Journal*, 15 August, 1767

13 p. 254 Barratt, W., *The History and Antiquities of the City of Bristol*, W. Pine, Bristol, 1789

14 pp. 10/11, Butcher, E.E., *Bristol Corporation of the Poor 1696-1834*, Bristol Record Society, 1982

15 Mishara, P., *The Guardian*, London, 11 November, 2017

16 pp. 49/50 Esquemeling, J., *The Buccaneers of America Reprinted from the First English Edition of 1684*, George Allen & Unwin, London, 1951

17 p.198, Jordan, D. and Walsh, M

18 p. 200, ditto

19 p. xv, Dame Paul, J.W

20 p. 1, Perkins, L., *The Evolution and Significance of a Chattel Slave Society: Virginia,   1619-1705,*   Confluences   2001 http://www.write.armstrong.edu/confluences/lp.html, 11/12/2006

21 p. 3, ditto

22 p. 5, ditto

23 p. 3, ditto

24 p. 5, ditto

25 ditto

26 p. 212, Jordan, D., and Walsh, M.

27 p. 131 Perkins, L.

28   https://mgmt6155ethics.blogspot.co.uk   Friday   March 02 2012

29   p.   2   http://yourarchives.national   archives.fov.uk/in-dex.php...Source_for_the_History... 18/05/2007

30 p. 152, Latimer, J.

31 p. 153 ditto

32 http://archiver.rootsweb.com/th/read/GERMANNA_COLONIE S/2004-09/1095041335 15/01/2007

33 p. 151, Latimer, J.

34 p. 144 ditto

35 pp. 1205–6 ditto

36 pp. 199–200 Barry, J., *The Diary of William Dyer: Bristol in 1762*, Bristol Record Society's Publication Vol. 64, Bristol, 2012

37 p. 30, McGrath, P., ed. *Merchants and Merchandise in Seventeenth Century Bristol*, Bristol Record Society vol. xix, Bristol, 1955

38 p. 27, Bowen, F.W.E., *Queen Elizabeth's Hospital, Bristol: The City School* Clevedon Printing, Clevedon, 1971

39 https://mgm6155ethics.blogspot.co.uk

40   www.danbyrnes.com.au/merchants/merchants8.htm 15/01/2007

41 Aylesbear-Azerly/BritishHistory Online www.britishhistory.org.uk/report... 50772 15/01/2007

42 Camden Hotten, J., ed., *Original Lists of Persons of Quality 1600-1700*, G.A. Baer & Co, New York, 1931

43 p. xvi, Latimer, J.

44 p. 89, Latimer, J., *Annals of Bristol Eighteenth Century, Vol. 2 Eighteenth Century*, George's, Bristol, 1970

45 p. 90, ditto

46 Bristol Record Office SMV/10/1/4/8

47 p. 306, Royster, C., *The Fabulous History of the Dismal Swamp Company: A Story of George Washington's Times*, Alfred A. Knopf, New York, 1999

Ch.4 Hanover Town

1 National Register of Historic Places Inventory – Nomination Form 10-300, Mechanicsville 06/19/1974

2 *Virginia Gazette*, 7 October 1737

3 p. 135, Latimer, J., *Annals of Bristol Eighteenth Century, Vol. 2 Eighteenth Century*, George's, Bristol, 1970

4 p. 1, www.co.hanover.va.us/history.htm

5 p. 8, Allen, B., ed., *The Faber Book of Exploration: An Anthology of Worlds Revealed by Explorers Through the Ages*, Faber and Faber, London, 2004

6 p.9 ditto

7 p. 131, Jordan, D., and Walsh, M., *White Cargo: The Forgotten History of Britain's White Slaves in America*, Mainstream, Edinburgh, 2007

8 p. 236, ditto

9 p. 3, *Virginia Gazette*, 15 April 1773

10 *Virginia Gazette* 4 February 1768

11 p. ix, McGrath, P., ed., *Bristol and the African Slave Trade to America vol. 1, The Years of Expansion 1698-1729*, Bristol Records Society, Bristol, 1980

12 p.393, Trevelyan, G.M., *English Social History A Survey of Six Centuries, Chaucer to Queen Victoria*, The Reprint Society, London, 1944

13 http://www.co.hanover.va.us/history.htm 10/25/2007

14 p.2, National Register of Historic Places Inventory – Nomination Form Hanover Town

15 p.35, vol. ii, Glazebrook, E.G. and P.G., compilers, *Virginia Migrations Hanover Country Vols I & II*, Clearfield Co., Baltimore, Maryland, 2002

16 p.30 vol. ii ditto

17 p.31 vol. ii ditto

18 p.32 vol. ii ditto

19 p.95 vol. ii ditto

20 *Virginia Gazette*, 15 April 1773

21 *Virginia Gazette*, 29 July 1776

22 p.3 *Virginia Gazette*, 15 July 1773

23 Hanover Town Archaeology, National Register of Historic Places Form 15-300

24 MS1 B9585a 2105 Virginia Historical Society

25 http://www.galantpelham.org/articles/showart 04/12/2006

Ch. 5 The Insurance Business

1 Kingsley N., *Country Houses of Gloucestershire, Vol. 2 1660-1830*,

2 p. 177, Pevsner, N., *The Englishness of English Art*, The Architectural Press, London, 1956

3 p. 327, Trevelyan, G.M., *English Social History A Survey of Six Centuries, Chaucer to Queen Victoria*, The Reprint Society, London, 1944

4 p. 328, ditto

5 p. 6, File 8 – 1700–1750 Merchants and Bankers Listings http://danbyrnes.com.au/merchants/merchants8.htm 15/01/2007

6 p. 7, ditto

7 p. 327, fn Trevelyan

8 p. 44, Flower, R., and Wynn Jones, M., *Lloyds of London: An Illustrated* History, David and Charles, Newton Abbot, 1974

9 p. 31, ditto

10 p. 5, File 8

11 p. 63, Flower, R. and Wynn Jones, M.

12 p. 50, ditto

13 p. 37, ditto

14 p. 63, ditto

15 p. 52, ditto
16 p. 59, ditto
17 p. 112, Royster, C., *The Fabulous History of the Dismal Swamp Company: A Story of George Washington's Times*, Alfred A. Knopf, New York, 1999
18 p. 264, ditto
19 p. 60, Flower, R., and Wynn Jones, M.
20 p. 66, ditto
21 p. 72, ditto
22 p. 72, ditto
23 p. 955, Barratt, W., *The History and Antiquities of the City of Bristol*, W. Pine, Bristol, 1789
24 Honourable and Loyal society of Ancient Britons wn.m.wikipedia.org
25 *Morning Chronicle*, 4 March 1809
26 *An Account of the Rise, Progress and State of the London Hospital From its institution on the 3rd of November 1740 to 1st January 1775, For the Relief of all Sick and Diseased Persons and in Particular Manufacturers, Seamen in Merchant Service and their Wives and Children* http://ota/ox-ac.uk/co/5567 via http://writersinspire.org/content/account-rise-progress-state-london-infirmary-supported-charitable-voluntary-subscription June 27 2018

Ch. 6 Gist's Will

1 p. 140, Royster, C., *The Fabulous History of the Dismal Swamp Company: A Story of George Washington's Times*, Alfred A. Knopf, New York, 1999
2 pp. 219, ditto
3 p. 411, Latimer, J., *Annals of Bristol Eighteenth Century, Vol. 2 Eighteenth Century*, George's, Bristol, 1970
4 pp. 446–7, Latimer, J.
5 p. 31, vol. ii, Glazebrook, E.G. and P.G., compilers, *Virginia Migrations Hanover County Vols I & II*, Clearfield Co., Baltimore, Maryland, 2002
6 www.bookrags.com/ebooks/13642/226.html 09/03/2007 The Journal of Negro History vol. 1, January 1916 eBook

7 Fairclough, K.R., Walton [nee Bourchier], Philippa (1674-1749) oxforddnb/.../48262 2017

8 p. 208, Royster, C.

9 p. 147, Jordan, D., and Walsh, M., *White Cargo: The Forgotten History of Britain's White Slaves in America*, Mainstream, Edinburgh, 2007

10 p. 218, Royster, C

11 p. 703, Barratt, W., *The History and Antiquities of the City of Bristol*, W. Pine, Bristol, 1789

12 p. 55, vol. ii, Glazebrook, E.G. and P.G.

Ch. 7 Manumission

1 Adeyemon, O., Part 8, *The Gist Settlements Research Project Report prepared for The National Underground Freedom Centre*, 15 July, 1999

2 p. 1, Untitled Document, Chapter 3: The Rationale of Fear http://negroartist.com/writings/The%20Rationale%20ofFear%20 in...13/03/2007

3 p. 207, Jordan, D., and Walsh, M., *White Cargo: The Forgotten History of Britain's White Slaves in America*, Mainstream, Edinburgh, 2007

4 www.mirandakaufman.com

5 p. 75, Latimer, J., *Annals of Bristol Eighteenth Century, Vol. 2 Eighteenth Century*, George's, Bristol, 1970

6 p. 212, Jordan, D., and Walsh, M.

7 p. 4, Untitled Document

8 p. 15, Villiers, A.J., *Convict Ships and Sailors*, Philip Allan, London, 1936

9 p. 7, Untitled Document

10 *Virginia Gazette*, 15 October 1772

11 *Virginia Gazette*, 18 March 1775

12 p. 149, Olusoga, D., *Black and British: A Forgotten History*, Pan, London, 2016

13 p. 162, ditto

14 p. 179, ditto

15 p. 194, ditto

16 p. 10, Untitled Document

17 p. 61, Burton, A., *The Rise & Fall of King Cotton*, André Deutsch/British Broadcasting Corporation, London, 1984

18 p. 62, ditto

19 http://www.lva.lib.va.us/whatwehave/gov/petitions/subjectresults. asp? 08/03/2007

20 p. 329, fn Shaffer, A.H., Ed., Randolph, E., *History of Virginia*, The Virginia Historical Society, The University of Virginia Press, Charlottesville, 1970

21 Brown County, Ohio *The Gist Settlement: Consequences of Manumission* http://home.aol.com/ugrrinfo/page36.html 08/03/2007 from Paul Young, *The Gist Settlement Book*, Brown Country Genealogical Society, Georgetown, 1997

22 www.lva.lib.va.us/whatwehave/gov/petitions/subjectresults.asp? 08/03/2007

23 page 8, National Historic Landmark Nomination, NPS Form 10-900, John P. Parker House

24 http://www.afrigeneas.com/slavedata/Anderson-VA-1789.html 08/12/2006

25 http://ancienttimes.blogspot.co.uk/2007/08/roman-slavery-and-the-rate-of-manumission.html

26 http://www.the-romans.eu/slavery/Manumission.php

27 Piercefield House, en.m.wikipedia.org

Ch. 9 Choosing the Land

1 p. 131, Schwarz, P.J., *Migrants Against Slavery: Virginians & The Nation*, University Press of Virginia, Charlottesville, 2001

2 African American History Heritage Travel & Tours http://creativefolk.com/travel/tours/ripley.html 04/12/2006

3 p. 131, Schwarz, P.J.

4 p. 213, McGroarty, W.B. *Exploration in Mass Emancipation*, William and Mary College Quarterly Historical Magazine, Vol. 21, No. 3 July 1941

5 www.co.hanover.va/us/history.htm 10/25/2007

6 p. 15, John P. Parker House, NPS Form 10-900 National Historic Landmark Nomination

7 p. 213, McGroarty, W.B.

8 p. 14, John Parker House

9 p. 13, ditto

10 p. 42, Young, P., *The Gist Settlement Book*, Brown County Genealogical Society, Georgetown, 1997

11 ditto

13 p. 2, Olding, M.A., Land Records for the Gist Settlement in Ohio, Draft Article for the Freedom Centre

15 p. 21, Wright, P.K.

14 p. 21, ditto

15 ditto

16 p. 4, Olding, M.A.

17 pp. 14–15, Wright, P.K.

18 p. 4, Olding, M.A.

19   http://omp.ohiolink/edu/OMP/Preview...   12/12/2007 Union Township Public Library

20 p. 34, Abdy, E.S., *A Journal of a Residence and Tour in the United States of North America From April 1833 to October 1834*, 3 vol.s, John Murray, 1835

21 p. 24, Wright, P.K.

22 p. 134, Schwarz, P.J.

23 p. 53, Young, P

24 pp. 37–8, Wright, P.K.

25 p. 37, ditto

26 p. 3, Schwarz. P.J.

27 p. 78, Abdy, E.S.

28 p. 217, McGroarty, W.B.

29 p. 224, ditto

30 Adeyemon, O., Part 8, *The Gist Settlements Research Project*, Prepared for the National Underground Railroad Freedom Centre, 15 July 1999

Ch. 10 Follow the Money

1 Isbell History by John R. Ward of the Isbells http://www.angelfire.com/va3/izzynet3/index1.html 14/03/2007

2 Virginia Historical Association MSS7:3 F225 7V1975:2

3 p. 40, vol. ii, Glazebrook, E.G. and P.G., compilers, *Virginia*

Migrations Hanover Country Vols I & II, Clearfield Co., Baltimore, Maryland, 2002
   4 ditto
   5 pp. 23–4, ditto
   6 https://unknownnolonger.virginiahistory.org
   7 p. 22, vol. ii, Glazebrook, E.G. and P.G.
   8 p. 20, Trotti, M., *The Execution of the Will of Samuel Gist: A Case Study of Private Manumission in Virginia*, Honors History Thesis, May 1, 1989, MSS 7:3 E185.18 T7566, Virginia Historical Society
   9 p. 21, ditto
   10 Mss2 T5757 a1, Virginia Historical Society
   11 MSS7:3 F225 7V1975:2 ditto
   12 p. ix, vol. ii, Glazebrook, E.G. and P.G.,
   13 p. 32, ditto
   14 *Virginia Gazette*, 15 April 1774
   15 p. 308, Royster, C., *The Fabulous History of the Dismal Swamp Company: A Story of George Washington's Times*, Alfred A. Knopf, New York, 1999
   16 p. 43, Trotti, M., The Execution ....
   17 p. 43, ditto
   18 p. 42, ditto
   19 p. 45, ditto
   20 p. x, vol. ii, Glazebrook,
   21 p. 135, Royster, C.
   22   http://wwww.gallantpelham.org/articles/showart... 04/12/2006
   23 p. 40, vol ii ,Glazebrook, E.G. and P.G.
   24 p. 39, ditto
   25 p. 30, ditto
   26 p. 33, ditto
   27 p. 28, ditto
   28 p, 29. ditto
   29 p, 15, ditto
   30 p. 36, ditto
   31 p. 31, ditto
   32 p. 35, ditto

33 p. 196, Royster, C.

34 p. 37, vol. ii, Glazebrook, E.G. and P.G.,

35 p. 21, ditto

36 p. 15, ditto

37 p. 17, ditto

38 p. 22, ditto

39 p. 21, ditto

40 p. 111, Royster, C.

42 p. vii, vol. ii, Glazebrook, E.G. and P.G.,

43 p. 43, ditto

Ch. 11 The Descent of Gist

1 *Morning Post,* 10 March 1815

2 *Bath Mirror,* 31 January 1818

3 *Morning Post,* 17 March 1815

4 Public Record Office Wills online

5 pp. 218–9, Royster, C., *The Fabulous History of the Dismal Swamp Company: A Story of George Washington's Times,* Alfred A. Knopf, New York, 1999

6 *Sheffield Independent,* 18 November 1826

7 www.epolix.com/EN/MPWebsites/Dai+Harvard/cadd/7449-f6b8... 15/01/2007

8 p. 24, Owen, W. and M., *Once Upon a Time in Merthyr Tydfil… The Birth and Growth of an Industrial Town,* W.B. and M.O. Owen, Merthyr Tydfil, 2018

9 p. 28, Owen, W., and M.,

10 p. 69, Latimer, J., *Annals of Bristol, Nineteenth Century,* W. & Morgan, Bristol, 1887

11 p. 70, ditto

12 Watson, J., *Savills A Family and a Firm 1652-1977,* Hutchinson Benham, London, 1977

13 p. 42, Owen, W. and M.

14 *Bristol Times & Mirror,* 25 April 1840

15 *Western Daily Press,* 28 November 1871

16 www.vauxhallcivicsociety.org.uk/history/brunswick-house

17 flikr

18 *Salisbury & Winchester Chronicle,* 23 November 1801

19 *Hampshire Telegraph*, 7 December 1801

20 Brown County, Ohio http:..home.aol.com/ugrrinfo/page36.html 08/03/2007

21 *Ipswich Journal*, 13 May 1826

22 *London Standard*, 11 May 1839

23 *Jackson's Oxford Journal*, September 23 1820

24 *Morning Post*, January 25 1820

25 *Morning Post* 28 March 1822

26 *Cheltenham Chronicle*, 27 August 1904

27 p. 45, Verey, D., ed., Wills, Ref. E.F., *The Diary of a Cotswold Parson*, Amberley, Stroud,. 2008

28 p. 89, fn ditto

29 p. 165, ditto

30 p. 55, Farr, G.E., *Records of Bristol Ships, 1800–1830 (vessels over 150 tons,)* Bristol Records Society, vol. XV, Bristol Record Society, J.W. Arrowsmith, Bristol, 1950

31 www.geneologyboard.com/gist/messages/1364.html

32 *Gentleman's Magazine*, 23 May 1806

33 *Gloucester Journal*, 21 August 1852

34 *Gloucester Journal*, 27 August 1904

Ch. 12 Gist's Legacy

1 p. 7, Bowen, F.W.E., *Queen Elizabeth's Hospital, Bristol The City School*, Clevedon Printing, Clevedon, 1971

2 p. 146, Nichols, J.E., and Taylor, J., *Bristol Past and Present, vol. II Ecclesiastical*, J.W. Arrowsmith, Bristol

3 earliest settlers.blogspot.co.uk

4 p. 6 will, Gist, Public Record Office wills online

5 Kingsley, N., *Country Houses of Gloucester*, vol. II 1660-1830

6 p. 102, Nichols, J.E., and Taylor, J.

7 Onuf, P.,S, Review, *The Fabulous History of the Dismal Swamp Company*, by Charles Royster, p. 625 *Journal of American History*, September 2001, University of Virginia, Charlottesville

APPENDIX II INDEX

Burke, Edmund 78
Byron, Commander 67
C
Carolina, South 93
Carr, John 10, William 10
Chancery, Court of, British, 101, 114, 166
Chantries 9
Chapel Royal choristers 132
Chapman, Maria Weston 125
Charles II 36
Chatterton, Thomas 16
Child actors 32
Children, abandoned in North America 18
Cinderella ix
Civil War, English,
American: see under war
Clark Township, Ohio 126
Clarkson, John 99; Thomas 90
Coalbrookdale 41, 162
Codrington, Christopher 74
Coffee houses 63, 64
Colliers, Kingswood 7
Colombus, Christopher 28
Colston, Edward 13, 14, 20, 45, 73, 120, 179, 182, 183, see also
under hospital Richard 45,
Committee for the Relief of the Black Poor 98
Cook, Captain James 11, 177
Coram, Captain 11, 177
Cornwallis, General 60
Cotton, cloth 56; factories 56; plants 100
Cromwell, Oliver 34, 35, 44, 192
Cruger, Henry 76, 77, 78
Cuffe, Captain Paul 116
Cyfarthfa iron works 161
D
Dampier, William 11, 53, 67, 71, 177

ABOUT THE AUTHOR

Barb Drummond climbs mountains to see past times. She burrows for hidden stories and lures them into the open to reveal their secrets. She asks why things happened, who was involved, how could they think it was a good idea. Sometimes she finds diamonds, or dust of things that mattered. She finds a single name, or a sentence, that lights up the sky like fireworks. Or she finds silence, which can also bear great meaning. She seeks patterns, themes, traces. Or shapes left by them. Sometimes she uses guesses to patch what is missing, but she makes it from the best possible material.

barbdrummond.co.uk
Twitter: @Barb_Drummond
Facebook: Barb Drummond

UNTITLED